ECONOMIC HISTORY

A BANKER'S WORLD

FINANCE, MONEY AND BANKING

A BANKER'S WORLD

The revival of the City 1957–1970, speakings and writings of Sir George Bolton

Edited by

RICHARD FRY

With a foreword by Sir Frank Lee

Routledge
Taylor & Francis Group
LONDON AND NEW YORK

First published in 1970

Published in 2006 by
Routledge
2 Park Square, Milton Park, Abingdon, Oxfordshire OX14 4RN
711 Third Avenue, New York, NY 10017

First issued in paperback 2014

Routledge is an imprint of the Taylor and Francis Group, an informa business

British Library Cataloguing in Publication Data
A CIP catalogue record for this book
is available from the British Library

A Banker's World
ISBN 0-415-38204-1 (volume)
ISBN 0-415-37850-8 (subset)
ISBN 0-415-28619-0 (set)

ISBN 13: 978-1-138-86521-1 (pbk)
ISBN 13: 978-0-415-38204-5 (hbk)

Routledge Library Editions: Economic History

A BANKER'S WORLD

The Revival of the City 1957-1970

Speeches and Writings of
SIR GEORGE BOLTON

Edited by Richard Fry
with a foreword by Sir Frank Lee

HUTCHINSON OF LONDON

HUTCHINSON & CO (Publishers) LTD
178-202 Great Portland Street, London W1

London Melbourne Sydney
Auckland Johannesburg Cape Town
and agencies throughout the world

First published 1970

ISBN 0 09 104960 1

CONTENTS

FOREWORD

It is difficult for me to imagine why I was invited to write this foreword, though I am happy to do so. The invitation was indeed an act of magnanimity, since a large part of my official life was spent in arguing violently with George Bolton. He thought me a timid bureaucrat. I thought him a reckless adventurer. I felt that his judgment of what policy we should follow on economic matters too often had only emphasis to commend it (*that* was never lacking): the one thing which I never doubted was the splendid and unfailing competence which he showed in carrying out whatever policy was adopted, whether he had opposed it or not.

Looking back, I feel now that we did not really differ about fundamentals but about timing. We both wanted to see an economy as free as possible of restrictions, where enterprise, risk-taking, and expertise would have full scope and a fair reward. His faith in our ability to move quickly to such a state of affairs was always more robust and optimistic than my own. I now think that for the most part he was probably right and I was wrong. Certainly the great achievements after he went to BOLSA, to which Mr. Fry pays tribute in his perceptive introduction and which had so stimulating an effect on the City, showed what the boy (and he always remained a boy in looks, resilience and obstinacy) could do when he was given his head and when circumstances allowed him to give full rein to his imagination and his great gifts as an operator on the market.

I feel sure that when we next meet we shall disagree violently and that I shall find myself saying, as so often in the past, "You're mad, George . . ." But at the same time I shall find myself remembering the phrase of another George—"Mad is he? I wish that he would bite some of my other generals . . ." George Bolton *has* bitten some of us, and to our great advantage. In a time of introspection, doubt, indecision, he had stood out splendidly as if from another age—resolute, high-spirited, dogmatic.

"One who never turned his back, but marched breast-forward,
Never doubted clouds would break . . .
Held, we fail to rise, are baffled to fight better,
Sleep, to wake . . ."

FRANK LEE

Introduction

THE REBIRTH OF THE CITY

In the decade of the sixties, which brought so many disappointments to the British people, one signal achievement stands out: the revival of "The City"—London's financial district—as a major centre of international finance. At the end of the fifties, London seemed to have been left behind in the progress of world trade and finance, first by the overwhelming resources of the United States, and more recently by the striking economic recovery of continental Europe. As a symbol of decline, many of the ragged gaps left by war-time bombing fifteen years earlier were still untouched, with pretty weeds flowering mauve and yellow each Spring among the rubble. The financial community was dominated by elderly men; seats on the Stock Exchange were sold cheaply; such was the prevailing pessimism that the sons of some bankers were training to be farmers. Tradition reigned and competition was considered respectable only within comfortably agreed limits.

That was the picture any intelligent visitor might have received. Yet the appearance was deceptive, and new life was already stirring beneath the crust. Within a few years the commercial and financial markets of the City had once more attracted a large and growing international business. There was an explosion of new building. A large number of American, Japanese and European banks hastened to open branches in the City or to forge links with British banks. Office rents within walking distance of the Bank of England shot up to well above the equivalent figures charged in Wall Street. By the close of the sixties the overseas funds deposited in London were equal to half the

British national income, and the net overseas earnings of the various services centred in the City—banking, insurance, merchanting, brokerage and shipping—were estimated at around £350 million a year (1968), compared with about £220 million in 1966 and only £125 million in 1956. (These figures are not strictly comparable but indicate the growth of London's financial earnings in broad terms. "The Banker" estimates that another £100 million should be added to the 1968 figure for export and import commissions.) These earnings went a long way to offset the country's deficit on merchandise trade in 1968, and their further rise in 1969 played a substantial part in turning the British balance of payments from deficit into surplus.

While the importance of these "invisible" earnings has lately attracted some attention, it is not generally appreciated that Finance has become Britain's most successful industry. In the long and painful struggle of the nation to regain a new economic balance after the loss of the Empire and the ravages of two world wars, such individual success counts for much. The achievement was utterly unexpected, and the process by which it was brought about is still little understood. It happened, after all, at a time when the role of the pound sterling in international trade and finance was rapidly declining. It happened in a period of almost incessant difficulties with the balance of payments and a widespread loss of confidence in the sterling currency.

Moreover, a powerful body of British opinion tended increasingly to criticise the use of sterling as an international trading and reserve currency and held this function responsible for the country's monetary troubles (Walter Bagehot, the famous economist, had made the same complaint a hundred years earlier in his book "Lombard Street", but without much effect). The Labour Government elected in 1964 was much influenced by this view. It imposed restrictions on overseas investment, revised the tax structure so as to discriminate against earnings from abroad, and even introduced a heavy new tax (the Selective Employment Tax) expressly designed to hold back "service industries"—which the country was said to be unable to afford—for the benefit of manufacturing industries.

It was against this hostile background that the City staged its comeback. A description of the main forces at work may be of interest. The London merchant banks, which after the second world war had concentrated largely on raising capital for British companies and helping them with financial advice in mergers and reconstructions, suddenly discovered around 1958 a new medium for international operations: the Euro-dollar. Some of the old British overseas banks, which were carrying on a local branch banking business in various parts of the world under increasing official restrictions, also grasped the opportunity offered by the mass of US dollars in non-American ownership to borrow and lend outside the reach of national controls. The old London commodity markets—coffee, cocoa, sugar, wool, the London Metal Exchange, rubber, vegetable oil, and many others—which had been successively reopened in the late forties and fifties, regained some of their international importance. The gold market, reopened in 1954, quickly became the largest in the world and remained so even when, in 1968, South Africa decided to make its sales of newly mined gold in Zurich rather than in London.

The London insurance industry, composed of a group of some 400 companies and the Lloyds Society of Underwriters, flanked by a number of powerful brokers, had been losing business to American, Swiss, and Japanese companies and was inclined, for a time, to blame inflation, high taxes, and nationalist restrictions abroad for its misfortunes. But about ten years ago, under pressure of losses, a process of rationalisation set in which yielded slow but promising results, and by 1970 London had regained some of its old pre-eminence as a world insurance centre. Elsewhere, several entirely new types of money market were created, offering a range of specialised services to international investors which, towards the end of the decade, was unequalled anywhere. The London Stock Exchange, always the only free and large stock market in Europe, underwent a rapid modernisation. Within a few years its dealing rules and requirements for financial information were tightened and the protection of shareholders greatly improved. As the investment of savings came increasingly into the hands of financial institutions, the techniques of investing were transformed, and a new generation of professionally trained investment analysts and managers emerged. One should perhaps mention that a similar process went on in financial journalism,. which played a considerable part in the modernisation of the City by providing an independent and incorruptible running commentary. If the best British merchant banks have few equals in the world, the "Financial Times" (to mention only one) has none. Press criticism was particularly active in demanding fair treatment for shareholders, and this led to the formation of the City "panel" on take-overs which, after some period of trial and error, took on far-reaching functions of supervision.

This is a brief outline. Two further points must be added to make the wider implications clear. One is the fact that the City has in recent years attracted a growing stream of the most enterprising young university graduates. Only a few years ago these men were much more likely to go into academic careers, the professions, the civil service or the more glamorous sectors of manufacturing. As late as 1965, few university careers advisers would mention Finance as a possible choice for a first-class honours student; it was regarded as having rather low social status, and it was seen to be unsuccessful and out of political favour. To appreciate the significance of the change, one must recall that British schools of all types tend to aim at preparing children for a civilised but "non-competitive" life, and that the teaching of both schools and universities almost unanimously looks upon profit-making as a rather unworthy occupation.

What has changed, in spite of these obstacles, is that the City is now a success, and that the success has enabled it to offer important incentives to young people. To work in the City now seems to hold the promise of moving up fast, not merely to good pay and good social standing but to an early share of responsibility. The merchant banks, the overseas banks, the specialised finance houses and the larger stockbrokers are so swamped with business that a bright newcomer may well get his hands onto real decision-making at a very early age. This prospect, and the general lowering of the City's average age, produce a spirit in which enterprise and inventiveness flourish.

The second point is the international reaction to the new role of the City. For various reasons finance has become more international in recent years: the rise of the multi-national business corporation requiring credit in a number of countries; the large pool of dollars deposited outside the U.S.A. as a result of the heavy payments deficits since 1958; the growing shortage of international liquidity in the traditional forms; the restrictions placed on capital outflow by the United States, which have compelled American and other corporations to seek capital in Europe. In response to this demand, vast liquid funds accumulated in twenty-five years of peace, prosperity and inflation by private individuals and financial institutions have been steadily drawn into the financial markets. All the major national authorities recoiled from the task of organising financial facilities to meet the new conditions. And while Finance Ministers and central banks argued over long-term plans to improve the world's payments system, and American officials urged the nations of the Common Market to open up their capital markets, the City of London quietly snatched the initiative.

Others, of course, did the same after a while, and a large business in the new international money and capital markets has grown up in Zurich, in Frankfurt, in Paris and in some other centres. The American banks, after a year or two in which some of their natural trade dominion was invaded by British rivals, returned to the fight and regained a lion's share of the market by setting up or expanding branches in London and other European capitals. But it was London that became the main focus, and for the present, at least, it is universally accepted throughout the capitalist world that London is the most important financial centre outside New York. The more American and other overseas banks opened offices in London, the more the international money flows gravitated to and through London. By the end of the decade about thirty U.S. banks had full branches in the City, and another twenty or so had linked with British banks in joint operations or by share participations.

Among other overseas banks the City harboured five Canadian, six Australian, twelve Japanese, five each from India and Pakistan, nine French, three Belgian, eight Italian, eight Swiss, four Spanish and a host of other banks. Altogether there were one hundred and thirty-five branches or representative offices of foreign banks in London, employing a total staff of ten thousand. The aggregate deposits of the foreign banks now exceed those of the British commercial (clearing) banks. Perhaps a small episode that occurred in 1969 may be said to have set the seal on the City's comeback: the seventh largest bank in the United States decided to transfer its entire international department from New York to London.

How did it happen? It is commonly said that the City simply applied its traditional skills to a new opportunity; that the banking structure and the technical experience survived when the sterling currency on which both had been based in the past lost its international utility. There is some truth in this, but it is not the whole truth. In 1957, when one of the periodic sterling crises led to another round of restrictions on oversea lending in sterling, and the first signs emerged that the long period of the world dollar shortage was ending, the City was ready to put two and two together. Why was it ready? How was it able to throw aside the paralysing effects of three decades of control and restriction?

It is not the real answer that "the old skills" were still alive. These skills had been gradually, deliberately re-awakened and refurbished by a succession of official acts, going back to the early post-war years. One of the earliest of these acts, which I remember well, was the raising of Bank Rate in November 1951 from two percent to two and a half percent, together with an indication from the Bank of England that changes in Bank Rate would in future be used as an instrument of monetary regulation—as they had not been used since June 1932 except for a brief interlude at the outbreak of war. In every London bank and discount house, the older men who could still remember how the system had worked twenty years earlier were called upon to explain it to the younger staff, and for some days the Bank's chief cashier, Sir Kenneth Peppiatt, was besieged by City men anxious to discover how to run a money market on a fluctuating base.

Similarly, as the tight exchange controls left over from the war were steadily loosened and many of the old City markets were allowed to reopen for international business, each new turn led to intensive technical discussions between the bankers and merchants concerned and officials at the Bank of England and the Treasury. Both sides made expensive mistakes, but the effort continued steadily. Throughout the fifties, the younger generation in the City was being trained in the "old skills" on a vague presumption that they would one day be needed again. It may be going too far to suggest that this amounted to a deliberate, farsighted policy, conceived mainly in the Bank of England and supported by a few of the most senior officials at the Treasury and Board of Trade; but there was undoubtedly a firm conviction that the financial and commercial service trades had something unique to contribute to the rebuilding of Britain's economic position in the world.

Policies, however, must be made effective by people. This is especially true when policies are permissive rather than mandatory. The City was merely given scope to develop profitable business; it was up to the bankers and traders to make the best of it. As it happened, there were in the City, at the end of the war, a number of enterprising men with bold ideas and technical ingenuity—men who refused to accept the apparent verdict of history that England no longer had the resources to run an important centre of world finance. One of these was Sir George Bolton, to whom this book is dedicated. The part he played in the rebuilding of the City was unique because, from 1948 until 1957, he was an executive director of the Bank of England, closely associated with the effort to restore the international role of the City; while after his retirement from executive work at the Bank, as chairman of the Bank of London and South America, he was one of the leading spirits in the creation of the new international money markets which gave London its chance.

There were others, of course. Looking back over the years when the City gradually rebuilt some of its old international business in the face of heavy discouragement, any close observer will be able to compose a list of men who were in the forefront of the effort. But I cannot imagine any such list of men which would omit the name of George Bolton. That is why this collection of his speeches and writings should be of more than biographical interest. The extracts cover the main period of the City revival, and quite apart from the personal views he expressed on many national and world issues, they convey something of the spirit which made this unexpected British triumph possible.

AT THE BANK OF ENGLAND

George Lewis French Bolton was born in 1900 and started work in the City before he was seventeen. He was trained as a foreign exchange dealer in the London branch of a French bank, the Société Générale de Paris. This was an exciting period in the foreign exchange market, when currencies fluctuated widely or collapsed altogether under the weight of post-war inflation. International speculation was heavy and many people—including eminent academics like John Maynard Keynes—made and lost vast fortunes buying and selling money which they never had. London was the undisputed centre of this market, and an active dealer was in constant touch with scores of banks around the world, making split-second calculations in his head (this is now done by computers) and taking instant decisions involving large sums. This work suited George Bolton; he has always recalled his early training as a dealer with pleasure and gratitude, and indeed it was the foundation of his professional success.

In 1920 he joined the merchant bank of Helbert Wagg & Co. (now incorporated in Schroder Wagg), where he stayed for twelve years, gaining experience in exchange and security arbitrage and seeing something of the discount and commodity markets, investment, new issues and international banking. In the main, he remained a foreign exchange specialist, and that led to the next turn of fortune. In 1931, the pound sterling was detached from gold and its exchange rate left to float. At first this caused a massive outflow of funds and the rate dropped from $4.80 to a low point of $3.25 at the end of December

1931. But soon confidence returned, the rate recovered, and funds began to flow back to London at such a rate that the Bank of England ran short of sterling with which to buy up foreign exchange.* So a new fund was formed, the Exchange Equalisation Account, designed to check "undue fluctuations in the exchange rate of sterling". The fund was controlled by the Treasury but operated by the Bank of England, an arrangement which has continued to the present day. At that time the Bank of England had very little experience of actual dealings in the foreign exchange market, which had always been left to a few specialised banks and brokers, while the Bank attended to the ultimate balancing of international accounts by transactions with other central banks. The Governor, Montagu (later Lord) Norman, decided to call in a number of experts from outside to build up a Foreign Exchange Department. Among these were Mr. Cameron Cobbold (later to be Governor himself, and now Lord Cobbold), Sir Charles Hambro of the banking family, Harry Siepmann from the Treasury, and as chief dealer, Robert Kay, who had come from Brown Shipley & Co. a year or two earlier. When the speculative pressures of 1932 made large-scale intervention by the Bank necessary, Kay needed an assistant. The Governor turned for advice to Nigel Campbell of Helbert Wagg, and his partner Albert Palache recommended George Bolton. Within a year or so Robert Kay collapsed and died in the street, and Bolton became head of the department, in charge of the management of sterling. That was to be his primary concern for over twenty years.

In a humorous after-dinner speech at the Fishmongers' Hall in 1959, Bolton gave his own version of these events: "Edward Holland-Martin has drawn attention to the coincidence that three persons here tonight—he, the Governor (Lord Cobbold) and myself—entered the services of the Bank of England about the same time. I feel I should make it clear that the three cases were not entirely similar. The first two I have mentioned came in through the front door in the full light of day, while I was smuggled through the wicket gate after dark to discuss foreign exchange—in those days a highly suspicious subject. I was eventually taken on for a short period to help in the formation of an office established to carry out the technical functions of the Exchange

* For a detailed account of this episode, see Bank of England Quarterly Bulletin, December, 1968.

Equalisation Fund. Within a few months, two-thirds of the American banks were closed down and America went off gold. Later, the elderly gentleman I had been recruited to assist dropped dead outside the Mansion House. The succession of shocks proved too much for the Bank and I stayed on by default rather than as the result of considered judgment."

Among those who worked with or for him in the thirties, several became leading figures in the City. Lord Cobbold has already been mentioned; he had gained international experience in France and Italy but he was probably brought into the Bank, not so much as a specialist, as to be groomed for the Governorship. His interest in the foreign aspects of the Bank's work, however, always remained strong, and as he rose to Deputy Governor and finally to Governor he relied much on Bolton's advice. Next, Sir Maurice Parsons, who at the time of Bolton's arrival was private secretary to Norman, worked closely with him on the international side for a quarter of a century. After the war, he succeeded Bolton first at the International Monetary Fund, then as Executive Director of the Bank of England, and after a spell as Deputy Governor he is now taking Bolton's place as chairman of the Bank of London and South America.

Two other names come to mind. In 1934, when Robert Kay died and Bolton became head of the foreign department, he took as his deputy Cyril Hawker (now Sir Cyril), a shrewd, quick-acting, cricket-playing young Bank of England official who himself rose to be Executive Director of the Bank and later became chairman of the Standard Bank, one of the surviving and successful British overseas banks. Finally, there was Roy Bridge, a bright young man in the dealing room whom Bolton picked out for promotion and trained with great care. Bridge became the Bank of England's chief foreign exchange operator and by the sixties was acknowledged throughout the international exchange markets as one of the most brilliant dealers in the world.

Apart from selecting his team well, one of Bolton's first acts after taking control was to clean up the London foreign exchange market, which during the currency chaos of the twenties had become overcrowded with brokers and agents, some of whom developed dishonest practices. At this time the big commercial banks which had in the past left foreign exchange operations to the specialists built up their own departments, and there was less need for a multitude of small brokers. The Bank of England was able to gain control of the market largely by channelling its own large operations only through houses of which it approved.

By the mid-thirties, after the devaluation of the dollar and the collapse of the continental "gold block", stability was again threatened by heavy flows of private funds in and out of different currencies—driven, in the main, by fears of oppression and war in Europe. Consultations between the Bank of England, the Bank of France and the Federal Reserve Bank of New York led to a plan for mutual aid in stabilising the three exchanges. The Tripartite Agreement to this effect was signed in 1936. It was, of course, an agreement between the three governments, but it had been negotiated mainly between central bank officials, among whom Charles Hambro, Harry Siepmann and George Bolton were prominent. By that time Bolton was engaged in international affairs at a high level, carrying much responsibility. He was working under a Governor, Montagu Norman, who had devoted himself since the early twenties to the rebuilding of a stable international payments system, and who always saw above these technical efforts the vision of world peace secured by financial co-operation. Norman's influence on all who worked under him at the Bank was enormous, and many of the ideas which George Bolton championed in later years bear the stamp of this influence.

By 1937 Norman (or Bolton, at any rate) became convinced that war was approaching. It was decided to prepare a mechanism of exchange control well in advance. Work began in great secrecy, with only a small group in the Foreign Exchange Department and one or two lawyers taking part. When war came, two years later, all the legal and technical requirements of exchange control had been thought out and provided for; and the scheme had been so devised as to apply to the entire Commonwealth, except for Canada which was economically tied to the United States. This was the origin of the official sterling area as it became known during and after the second world war. All the Commonwealth countries whose currencies were linked with sterling, with the addition of Iran, Iraq and a few other territories, agreed to restrict the use of gold and non-sterling currencies by their nationals, to pool their foreign exchange earnings in London, and to maintain consultation with the Bank of England on the working of these far-reaching and complex controls. The document containing the complete machinery of war-time exchange control, with detailed regulations for different markets and sections of business, was ready three weeks before war was declared. In the remaining spell about one hundred officials of the Treasury and Bank of England were called in to be intensively briefed on the operation of the controls, and on the day the Germans invaded Poland they were ready to start operations.

A fuller description of pre-war and wartime activities at the Bank of England, including the printing of a new note issue and the secret shipment overseas of gold and securities, was given by Bolton himself in a talk to naval officers in 1963. The relevant passages will be found on page 111.

It was strange that the task of planning and supervising the war-time exchange control system fell to George Bolton, who hated bureaucratic controls and interference with the business of the markets. But the job had to be done, and he did it. However, he did what he could to humanise the scheme. Its basic principle was very simple: any payment for "current" transactions was allowed; any payment of a "capital" nature was forbidden unless specially passed. In practice, any bona fide proposition involving mainly current payments for goods and services was almost invariably permitted, and the financial community was given considerable scope for business so long as the Control was told the truth. As for Bolton's own part in it, a former colleague recalls: "Administering regulations was not his strong point. He disliked them too much. But he was superb as a generator of ideas. George would produce schemes, suggestions, proposals as a machine gun spits bullets. If the technical people turned down one of his schemes as impracticable, he yielded at once and was ready with a new one."

Another colleague, still at the Bank of England, put this in a wider context: "Bolton was never really a part of the institution. He remained a market man, a dealer at heart, but of course he was much more than a dealer. He had little patience for the routine answer and took little interest in the machinery. But he had a rare capacity for vision, for looking into the future. His was a strong personality; you had to be pretty determined to make your own views heard when he was about. He always speaks with deep conviction; he is interested in human motives, in the consequences of policies for mankind. That, and his intense interest in history and world affairs, probably explain his taste for sweeping statements—a taste that has sometimes frightened off the more pedantic officials he was trying to win over."

The same affectionate criticism comes from yet another former associate: "Bolton's habit of over-emphasis may have provoked defensive reactions in Whitehall." It certainly did. Even those few among the senior government servants who shared Bolton's concern for the preservation of the financial structure were often upset by his habit of speaking bluntly about people and policies, regardless of any feelings that might be hurt. Still, they would always agree that Bolton, from his key position at the Bank, had made a powerful contribution to the war effort. Indeed one member of the War Cabinet let it be known that in his opinion George Bolton had done more than most others to bring the country safely through the war.

In 1942, when Harry Siepmann retired, Bolton succeeded him as Adviser to the Governors on exchange and monetary policy. In that position he became deeply involved in the plans for constructing the post-war system of international payments which resulted in the formation of the International Monetary Fund and the World Bank. He was adviser to the U.K. delegation at the Bretton Woods conference in 1944—in fact he was the only official present with practical knowledge of currency markets. Both at Bretton Woods and at the Savannah Conference in 1945, and again during the painful negotiations on the United States loan to Britain, Bolton attended as an expert adviser, overshadowed not only by Ministers but by the towering prestige of J. M. Keynes. It is no secret that the settlement which emerged from all these meetings was not the one the British side would have liked; and Bolton has often criticised various aspects of it.

But in one respect the British got their way: they rejected the American proposal that the wartime "sterling balances" should be scaled down and funded into long-term liabilities. The chief British motive was a general fear that the post-war years would bring another world slump, similar to that of the twenties, and that in these conditions it might be useful to have a great mass of purchasing power, tied to purchases of British goods, in the hands of Indians, Egyptians, East Africans and many other nations. To this view Bolton may well have added his own belief that it would be possible to restore the international role of sterling, and that, once this had been done, the "debts" would simply become deposits in London banks, safe and sound as long as confidence was not disturbed.

But if Bolton had reservations about the Bretton Woods agreements he took a very active part in making them work. In 1946 he was made the first U.K. director of the I.M.F., a post in which he spent much time in Washington until 1952 and had considerable influence on the formative years of the Fund. In 1948 he was appointed Executive Director of the Bank of England and in 1952 he became Alternate U.K. Governor of the I.M.F. During this period he attended every international monetary conference on behalf of the Bank of England, including all the Commonwealth Conferences in which the maintenance of the sterling area played an increasingly controversial part.

Much of his attention, during the same period, was devoted to European problems. He had followed events on the continent both during and after the war very closely and was deeply concerned in concrete financial arrangements. The war in Europe was not yet over when he began to negotiate a series of monetary agreements with the emerging post-war governments in Western Europe; in those early days of economic and social chaos these agreements, very generous from the British side, laid the foundation for European recovery well before the Marshall Plan came into action. Next, Bolton helped to devise the first European Payments Union which transformed the network of bilateral payments agreements between European nations into a single monetary system. The same objectives led the Bank of England to promote the restoration of the Bank for International Settlements in Basle, and in 1949 Bolton became a director of that Bank which played an increasing part in restoring free markets in Europe and in building up co-operation between central banks.

While Western Europe gradually regained economic health the British position deteriorated. The brief attempt to make the pound convertible in 1947—made prematurely, on Amercian insistence, at a time when the rest of the world was starving for dollars—led to the loss of the U.S. loan proceeds almost overnight. A belated effort to reduce or fund the sterling liabilities failed utterly. Both these undertakings were bungled to a degree that can only be explained by the general bewilderment of people suddenly confronted with the almost forgotten problems of peace. The wartime sterling balances were in fact drawn down so fast that they could not possibly be met from the reduced and damaged British resources; they were fortuitously replaced after a time by new balances resulting from the oil discoveries in the Middle East.

The Korean War inflicted more economic damage on Britain than on any other nation involved. Not only did it cause steep price rises in food and raw materials which Britain had to import to live, but the British Government was induced to commit itself to a heavy rearmament programme which overburdened the British economy for years to come. The countries which as members of the sterling area had undertaken to pool their foreign exchange earnings in London now drifted themselves into deficit and called on London for dollars. In 1949 the central reserves had fallen away to a point where the pound had to be devalued. For a time things improved. But by 1951 the new Conservative Government of which Sir Winston Churchill was again the head and Mr. R. A. (now Lord) Butler was Chancellor of the Exchequer had once more to face a dangerous outflow of reserves.

A number of Ministers—Butler himself, Sir Oliver Lyttelton (who had hoped to be Chancellor, and had prepared ideas for the task) and some others—were determined not to meet the crisis with the same methods of retrenchment and austerity that they had criticised when their socialist predecessors used them. They planned a "dash for freedom", and their hopes were met by a proposal worked out by officials of the Bank of England and the Treasury: the pound was to be made convertible for non-residents of the sterling area on a floating exchange rate; and for a time, the greater part of the existing sterling balances (90 per cent of private and at least 80 per cent of official balances) were to be blocked. The plan went under the code name ROBOT, taken from the names of its three authors: Sir Leslie Rowan, Sir George Bolton, and Sir Richard (known universally as "Otto") Clarke.

ROBOT was debated among officials and in the Cabinet with great persistence and much heat. Governor Cobbold was a strong advocate, and Chancellor Butler tried hard to win over the Prime Minister. But there were two powerful opponents, both old wartime intimates of Churchill, who had his ear: Lord Cherwell (Professor Lindemann) and Lord Salter. Cherwell argued day and night that a floating exchange rate would sink the pound and that blocking the balances would be seen as a plain default. Salter, who was Economic Secretary to the Treasury, thought the policy would result in "a great national disaster". Churchill himself was haunted by memories of 1925, when as Chancellor of the Exchequer he had been persuaded by a similar group of officials to restore something like the gold standard and to bring the pound back to its pre-war parity of $4.82, which turned out to be too high for British Industry to live with. As Salter tells the story, Churchill finally rejected ROBOT at a last Cabinet meeting because "I can't help feeling that when Cherwell and Salter agree there must be something in what they say."

The ROBOT controversy has been described in some detail in two books: Lord Birkenhead's biography of Lord Cherwell, "The Prof. in Two Worlds" (Collins, 1961) and Lord Salter's "Slave of the Lamp" (Weidenfeld & Nicolson, 1967). The decisive argument advanced against the scheme was that in view of the world-wide dollar shortage other countries would discriminate against British exports so as to earn more sterling which they would convert into dollars. It was also argued that, in practice, more reserves would be needed to manage a floating exchange rate than to defend a fixed rate. Butler did not accept this: "We want to be able to use the rate as well as the reserves" he explained; and he believed this would ease the strain on both.

The idea that a solution of the British difficulties ought to be sought in greater freedom of markets rather than in more and more restriction did not die when ROBOT was defeated. "In August 1952", writes Lord Birkenhead, "yet another version of the convertibility scheme was bitterly argued between various departments". This time it assumed a "collective approach":—several other European countries were to be persuaded to make their currencies convertible at the same time. When Butler put the idea to a meeting in Paris it was as if he had stepped into a hornets' nest; he had to hurry back to London to assure Parliament that he had meant nothing of the sort, and the flight from the pound did not stop until the following month when he gave a formal pledge at the annual meeting of the I.M.F. that the parity of the pound would remain fixed and unaltered.

The movement towards monetary freedom, however, continued in less open forms. In August 1952, it was decided to try an experiment in widening the scope of the London commodity markets. It seemed a small matter: European traders were to be allowed to buy "dollar" commodities in London, and arbitrage was permitted on this basis.

The rush to get dollars for pounds by this back door was so great that the scheme had to be hurriedly abandoned. A much more cautious process of broadening commodity dealings began in 1954, when arbitrage in dollar commodities was kept under strict control. Meanwhile a limited approach to convertibility of payments was tried out. Sterling earned within any of the four or five dozen separate payments agreements was made "transferable" for payments within the whole of this trading area. Gradually, over several years, "transferable sterling" became a useful international currency in a fairly large part of the world which had no other practical means of payment, as U.S. dollars were still too scarce to serve that purpose.

In February 1955, the Bank of England at last won the substance of its convertibility ideal: it obtained permission to support the rate for transferable sterling by intervening in the Zurich market. It proved possible, by making skilful use of the balancing financial movements of the many currencies involved, to maintain the rate for transferable sterling very close to that for official sterling, and on that basis the pressures which had beset the pound before gradually subsided. International commodity trading was steadily resumed in London. Exchange control was liberalised during 1955 and 1956, and the effort to make the major currencies of the world convertible for purposes of trade and current payments could be resumed in earnest. The Suez affair and the sterling crisis that followed delayed agreement on convertibility for nearly two years. By that time the main practical difficulty, the world-wide shortage of dollars, had been largely removed by a series of U.S. payments deficits. Finally, at Christmas 1958, eleven governments accepted the convertibility obligations laid down by the I.M.F.

Bolton did not wait for the victory. He had been wholeheartedly behind the "dash for freedom" policy in 1952 and was deeply disappointed when it was frustrated. For another five years he supervised the gradual advance towards convertibility at the Bank of England, pressing all the time for the lightening of controls and the re-opening of City markets, and encouraging bankers and merchants to look out for foreign business. But he found less and less scope for creative action at the central bank, and he was probably ready to move when the suggestion came that he should take the chairmanship of the Bank of London and South America and, in his own words, "to see what could be done to prevent any further decline of British influence in this large and important part of the world".

In fact, he knew very well that the battle for the preservation of sterling as a world currency had been lost. Thirteen years later he revealed* that one of his first major decisions on joining BOLSA was to prepare "a deliberate withdrawal from sterling activities in the belief that the international use of sterling would virtually cease". The conviction that the sterling system in which the British overseas banks had been operating was about to disintegrate led him to "convert BOLSA from a regional bank to an international bank", and it was the basis of his search for dollar deposits which was one of the earliest roots of the Euro-dollar market. It was also the real motive for his departure from the Bank of England. Like most enterprising people, Bolton was only interested in his work when there was a campaign to be fought. With either victory or defeat his interest waned—until a fresh cause emerged.

* In an interview with "The Banker" of February 1970

DAWN OF A NEW ERA

In 1957, when Bolton left the Bank of England to join BOLSA, the City showed few outward signs of the coming revival. Banks of all kinds were mainly concerned with domestic business, which was profitable as British production expanded and the structure of industry changed rapidly. The insurance industry had hardly begun the great reorganisation which got underway in the later sixties and is still incomplete. The port of London, always an important part of the City's financial system, was being overtaken by the growing ports of the continent. It is true that the foreign exchange and gold markets had managed to become fully international despite restrictions on the use of sterling. The (short-term) Money Market, which had earlier been reduced to employing the daily surplus cash of the commercial banks in government bills and bonds, turned a corner in 1955 when the Treasury directed the Local Authorities to borrow in the open market at the going rate of interest: deposits with British Local Authorities, dated from seven days to a year, and virtually guaranteed by the Treasury, became a convenient international medium for holding temporary cash balances, and a number of London money brokers quickly organised an efficient international market. In 1958 the Radcliffe Committee, enquiring into the monetary system, discovered the beginnings of the "parallel money markets" which became so important a few years later. But its Report of 1959 dwells more on the inadequacies of the monetary machine from the Government's point of view than on its potential strength as a British export industry.

A few people sensed the turn of the current. Throughout 1958 intensive negotiations went on between central banks and the International Monetary Fund to clear the way to making the main currencies convertible into each other and into dollars, at least for "external" purposes. By Christmas 1958, eleven countries joined in a declaration of convertibility. Exchange control was lifted from current payments and liberalised on capital payments. "It was to be the dawn of a new era" said a London merchant banker, looking back; "We thought it was the end of the siege economy that had been operated since 1939. Certainly it was the culmination of the devoted work of all those who believed in Freedom. And while these hopes were not fulfilled, mainly because the sterling position began to deteriorate again in 1961, the 1958 agreement was a milestone in the progress of the City."

It was not only the renewed weakness of sterling that dimmed the fair vision of 1958; it was also the transformation in the status of the American dollar. The balance of payments of the United States had swung abruptly from surplus into deficit as early as the fourth quarter of 1949, after the devaluation of sterling in September of that year. But for a number of years the deficits were relatively small and the outflow of dollars and gold which resulted served only to relieve what had been a desperate shortage of both in the rest of the world. But in 1957–58 the U.S. deficit became so large that American dollars began to be plentiful in Europe. Just as the pound sterling became more difficult to use as an international trading and financing currency, the dollar became at last ready to take its place.

The change-over did not happen overnight. It was set in motion by some London banks for two reasons. One, new restrictions put on the use of sterling in 1957 to finance trade between "third countries";*

* Bank of England rules for the use of the London Bill to finance shipments of goods to and from countries outside the sterling area were changed several times, and these changes greatly affected the business of the City. In 1954, banks were permitted to grant credit up to one hundred and twenty days for trade not touching the U.K. In addition, a practice grew up of re-financing in sterling the shipment of goods from the sterling area where the buyer paid the seller in cash but covered himself by raising a bill credit in London. Both practices were stopped by an Exchange Control rule in September 1957. Early in 1959, the ban was lifted in part, and in 1960 certain types of trade credit up to six months were again allowed. In 1962 the restrictions were removed on the refinance by non-residents of purchases from the sterling area, and this facility is still open. However, in October 1968 permission to finance trade between non-sterling area

the other, the commercial advantage of British over American banks in the traditional spread between borrowing and lending rates. The second point is of fundamental importance, both in explaining the past and in judging the future. Banks in the United States, limited by an official ceiling in the interest rates they can offer for deposits, charge their customers not only the quoted loan rates but add a heavy surcharge by demanding that the borrower draws the entire loan at once and re-deposits between fifteen and twenty per cent on a current account, free of interest. The British custom of granting overdraft facilities and charging interest only on amounts drawn means that London banks can always "get between" the New York rates for almost any credit transaction. From 1957 onward they made use of this difference in offering holders of dollars in Europe and elsewhere higher rates than were obtainable in the United States. There is no reason to fear that the City will lose this advantage of cheapness if and when American conditions change, either through the ending of restrictions on U.S. overseas lending, or through the abolition of the deposit rate ceiling laid down in "regulation Q".

It was in day-to-day dealings with money that a new discovery was made: the financial organisation of the City, with its world-wide connections built up in the age of sterling predominance, might survive even if the sterling system did not. Perhaps an efficient banking structure and a pool of highly-trained financial specialists might be more important than the medium in which they operated. Just how the first international dealings in dollars owned outside the United States grew into a vast new international market is difficult to trace; but at the beginning there was a real need for such a medium both on the supply and on the demand side. It is generally agreed that one of the earliest factors was the Banque Commerciale de l'Europe du Nord (cable address: "EUROBANK"), a Soviet-owned bank in Paris used by a number of communist countries to finance east-west trade, together with its London sister unit, the Moscow Narodny Bank. They held substantial working balances; the troubles of sterling had made them nervous of holding much money in pounds, and the political tensions of the cold war made them fearful that dollar deposits

countries was once more withdrawn. London banks can now finance this trade only through the Eurodollar market; the international use of sterling has been decisively curtailed.

in American banks might one day be blocked. An attempt to move into Swiss francs was given up after a horrified intervention by the Swiss central bank. What was wanted was a reliable non-American bank which would borrow the dollars and undertake to repay them in dollars.

The very idea occurred to some bankers in the City of London around the same time. Sir George Bolton, when he moved from the Bank of England to BOLSA, looked for a new medium to replace sterling in the bank's international activities. One of his first acts had been to set up a new foreign exchange department; the dealers were told to look for deposits in foreign currencies, to be used for transactions in Latin America and in Europe. They found dollars looking for a borrower. "In September 1957", says one of them, "we started to canvas banking connections and other correspondents in continental Europe for dollar deposits and we very quickly began to collect funds once it was realised that we were paying realistic and worthwhile rates in excess of the going rate in New York."

No doubt this is a grossly over-simplified version of Euro-dollar history. Others grasped the opportunities around the same time. What is certain is that Bolton was one of the first to plunge headlong into the new medium, and that for several years BOLSA was the largest single dealer in Euro-dollars in London. The business increased quickly. Almost at once Bolton turned the bank's offices in New York and Zurich into catchment vessels for dollars (and other currencies) owned by Latin Americans and Europeans. At first the dollars were both borrowed and lent for short periods, but gradually the deposits were used as a basis of slightly longer and even medium-term lending. That led to some losses when interest rates rose unexpectedly, but over the years it was a highly profitable business. After 1963 when the New York capital market was virtually closed to foreign borrowers a European bond market in dollars (and later in D-marks) developed. This, too, was initiated by London banks, and BOLSA captured a share in it, especially in the secondary market in Euro-bonds already in issue. For a more detailed account of the Euro-dollar market—or international money market, as it should now be called—the reader should turn to Bolton's own analysis on pages 142–152 of this book.

Having returned to private banking in the City at this crucial moment in its history, Bolton found BOLSA, as an outsider put it, "a wonderful old vehicle in a state of disuse". It had been put together by a merger of four British banks in Latin America in 1936, when Lloyds Bank was brought in as a major shareholder. With the general decline of the British position in Latin America, and the sequence of local restrictions, defaults, and currency crises, the business of the bank had languished. Many branches were closed down, in Spain and Portugal as well as throughout Latin America. Competition from domestic banks in the various countries had become very strong, and American banks had grown aggressive. Yet the chief weight of BOLSA was in the branch network rather than at the London centre. In these circumstances the bank had run short of capital and failed to renew its ageing staff. A new effort was signalled, even before Bolton arrived, by the decision to raise new capital and to put up a large new building in London, but the pace of change was at first slow.

One has to recall this situation in such realistic terms in order to appreciate the changes which followed Bolton's succession to the chairmanship. Within a year or two a number of younger men were promoted to managerial posts; the recruiting of talented young men which had been started by the previous chairman, Sir Francis Glyn, was accelerated; and a decision was taken to embark on a huge rebuilding programme in Europe and Latin America. As soon as the drive to attract Euro-dollar deposits began to bear fruit, an international banking division was formed whose main task was to offer medium-term finance to Latin American governments and international companies. Relations with eastern Europe was actively developed. BOLSA went into the under-writing and selling of Euro-bonds. In Latin America, Bolton set out to move from the financing of trade and the lending of working capital to the support of local long-term development. All this promised to grow into big business, but it could not for long rest on such dollars as BOLSA could borrow in the money market. A more secure access to large dollar resources was needed. Bolton decided early that BOLSA had to become an Anglo-American bank. Firm links were forged, first with the Bank of Montreal, and later with the Mellon Bank of Pittsburg. The plan succeeded, and it was typical not only of Bolton's forceful tactics but of the general readiness of the City at that time to seize a new place in a new kind of world.

It would be pleasant to think that the City snatched success out of defeat by sheer daring and skill; but that picture, though popular, is overdrawn. As the world of industrial corporations and, as a consequence, of banking became more international, a centre like London, located halfway between America and Europe in terms of jet travel, telephone, cable and telex services, and language, had important advantages. London lies today within a non-stop jetliner trip of the capitals of more than ninety per cent of the developed world. These objective advantages might have applied, except for language, to Paris or Frankfurt as much as to London, but they were backed in the City by a traditional tolerance of foreign competition, by laws and regulations giving easy access to markets, and by a central bank anxious to help any private enterprise that might make some contribution to the country's business. One must not overlook that the Bank of England provided the facilities for the development of the new international money market at a time when almost all other monetary authorities were fearful of the credit risks involved, and of the loss of national control over interest rates and over the movement of funds which did, in fact, follow.

In addition, of course, the City had a unique reservoir of trained foreign exchange dealers and managers, accountants, tax experts and other specialists, all of them accustomed to the strangely informal and trusting ways in which the City does its business. When the American and other foreign banks began to pour into London during the sixties they were able to engage ready-made local staff—though in the process they pushed up the level of salaries, and of office rents, to unprecedented heights. Thus the revival of the City was based on an amalgam of technical, social and human factors. The upshot is that the City survived the shock of sterling devaluation in 1967 despite the heavy losses suffered by some of the banks and commodity merchants, and emerged as the leading financial centre outside New York.

Bolton's part in these developments was substantial, both by his own work and by the inspiration he gave to others. But his own horizon went far beyond the concerns of the City. As his speeches and writings bring out, he was always forming views on world-wide conditions and trends, and trying to assess what Britain ought to do to make the best of its opportunities. Many events outside the field of finance engaged his interest. In 1958 the European Common Market was formed without British participation. Bolton had favoured close co-operation with Europe but was repelled by the supra-national and bureaucratic aspects of the Rome Treaty. He had spent much of the post-war period in the United States; after 1957 he paid extensive visits to Latin America and was immensely impressed by the scope offered by that region. In his long fight to preserve the international sterling system he had grown accustomed to looking at the world as a whole. In that perspective, the small area of Western and Southern Europe covered by the Common Market dwindled in size and importance. Bolton steadily moved towards the view that Britain had little to expect from joining the European Community, and less by concerning herself deeply with Asia and Africa. It was in some kind of association with North and South America—a "Western" rather than an "Eastern" policy—that he saw the most promising pattern of the future. This view culminated in the London study of the implications of a North Atlantic Free Trade Area (NAFTA) in which he took an active part. These ideas are set out, as they developed, in a number of the speeches and papers reproduced later in this book.

Bolton's first few years in commercial banking were marked by a succession of world-shaking events which he was forever seeking to foresee and interpret. 1958 saw not only the formation of the E.E.C. but Krushchev and de Gaulle lifted to supreme power and, on a lesser scale, currency convertibility achieved. In 1959, Castro seized power in Cuba, and the first Russian rocket reached the moon. In 1960, the main news came out of Africa: revolt in the Congo, and the start of the great British and French withdrawals from all colonial positions. The year closed with the election of President Kennedy. It was also notable for the first eruption of the international monetary crisis, variously described as a flight into gold, a weakening of the dollar, or a basic shortage of "liquidity" to finance the continuing growth of world production and trade.

These were the kind of events that provoked Bolton to look for the underlying truth. His comments were not those of a detached philosopher; he was actively engaged in his daily task and wanted above all to see where he was going, and where his country was heading, so that he might influence policy. It is in this sense that his views over these twelve years should be read. Some of the extracts reproduced show him to have been wrong in some of his hopes and fears; he has never been afraid to form a view and never waited until he was sure of knowing how the wind blew. This willingness to speak out, to take a line, to differ from the collective view may be the quality which, above all, gained him the respect and affection of the financial community throughout the world.

The impression he made on others in the City is reflected in the following note from Sir Siegmund Warburg, the merchant banker.

"I first met George Bolton two or three years before the last war when he was in the foreign exchange department of the Bank of England. The immediate impression he made on me was based on the wonderfully clear cut and decisive way in which he put forward his views. There was nothing ambiguous or half-hearted about the attitudes he took. Strong principles and consistent conclusions from these principles were evident in everything he said. Nothing has changed in this respect during more than three decades.

"In our frequent discussions we disagreed often and strongly in our judgment of people and on matters of international and domestic policy, as well as on monetary problems. However, I have always had to respect not only the intellectual strength behind his arguments but above all his personal and strongly emotional involvement in the statements he makes and the moral fervour with which he propounds his opinions.

"Possibly of all his many remarkable qualities it is this moral fervour which is at the core of George Bolton. However strong his sense of reality—and he is certainly not a wishful thinker—he is an idealist through and through, serving single-mindedly the aims in which he believes.

"At the end of the war, in addition to working for the revival of close relations between the central banks of the western world, he gave much encouragement to private houses in the City to build up international business from London notwithstanding foreign exchange regulations and many other impediments. His influence always favoured individual endeavours as distinct from the more anonymous powers of the state machinery, and equally those who tried to open new, privately-based channels for international co-operation.

"During the first two decades after the war many sceptical observers felt that owing to the numerous sterling crises and particularly due to the fact that Britain had changed from a creditor nation into a debtor nation London would gradually lose its position as an important international financial centre. It was the British talent for improvisation and the British eagerness to take reasonable risks which were the main factors in making London once more the most important financial centre in Europe—though, contrary to its role at the beginning of this century, rather an entrepot and intermediary centre than one providing capital out of its own funds. It was the merit of a few leaders, among whom George Bolton was one of the foremost, that London regained and maintained this leading position.

"The attitude of a merchant adventurer which characterised many of George Bolton's actions at the Bank of England found its strongest expression when he became head of the Bank of London & South America. What he has done there proves that however big and complicated a business enterprise may be, the courage and vigour of one man can change the spirit throughout a large organisation.

"In mentioning some of these examples of George Bolton's activities I have possibly not done sufficient justice to his initiatives outside the financial sphere, in particular his efforts to intensify relations with the continent of Europe and with countries on the other side of the Iron Curtain. Although George Bolton has never been in favour of Britain joining the Common Market—a subject on which I disagreed with him during the years preceding the Rome Treaty—he has always been an ardent European.

"In conclusion I should like to say that George Bolton has one gift above all others, namely a gift for friendship. His loyalty to his friends is never that of a yes-man but is the best of loyalties, that of a man who has the courage to speak the truth to his friends, however unpleasant it may be, and to stand by them even more in bad than in good weather.

"Examples are worth more than precepts. George Bolton's example of courage and loyalty is a star shining brightly and constantly for his friends."

But a man who makes such friends is bound to make enemies as well. Bolton has been actively involved in many bitter controversies. In preparing this book I have come across a striking variety of attitudes among people with whom he has disagreed from time to time. I will mention two remarks, both from civil servants, which indicate the extreme range of his impact on others. "We regarded him as a little mad", says one who was on the opposite side of the convertibility argument in 1952.

Another, more eminent, who met Sir George frequently over a period of years, said this: "He has been one of the primary forces of our time."

Speeches and Writings, 1956-1970

THE HORRORS OF PEACE

In 1956, when Bolton was still at the Bank of England, he made a speech explaining the role of sterling and the sterling system in the world. As this was the foundation of his work for many years, he spoke with much authority, and his warning that the failure of the system might mean "a collapse of civilisation as we know it" reflects his fears that the end was already in sight.

The problem of confidence in sterling is a matter of far greater importance than is generally understood. You may often have heard that more than half of the world's trade is settled in sterling and this is roughly true. But this phrase cloaks the more important fact that a very large part of the Western World depends on our money to maintain the value of their own currencies. The Australian pound, the Indian rupee, the Hong Kong dollar, the Malayan dollar, the East and West African shilling, the Rhodesian pound, the British West Indies dollar, the Egyptian pound, the Iraqi dinar and a score of other currencies are either pegged to sterling or depend substantially for their value in trade and finance on sterling. This means, for example, that a very large proportion of the trade and finance of Africa south of the Sahara, the exceptions being the Belgian Congo and the Portuguese Colonies, is directly and indirectly dependent upon the stability of sterling. The largest oil reserves available to the world are in the Persian Gulf area and nearly the whole of the oil produced in Persia, Iraq, Kuwait, Saudi Arabia, etc. is sold for sterling irrespective of whether the producing companies are controlled from London, New York or other foreign capitals. The sub-continent of what used to be called Undivided India trades externally and internally in currencies which are in practice, if not legally, interchangeable with sterling. The currencies of Singapore and Hongkong which serve to finance the bulk of the trade in the China Seas can only be created against the deposit of sterling. The economic and political system, therefore, of hundreds of millions of people depends directly and indirectly on sterling being a good and useful currency.

This situation can be illustrated by figures: cash balances of sterling held outside the U.K. total about £3,750 million, of which, say, £3,000 million represent sterling held as reserves by countries in the sterling system. The balance of £750 million represents balances held by the rest of the world largely to finance foreign trade. Against these sterling liabilities we hold about £800 million of gold and foreign exchange. This figure is clearly inadequate to meet anything more than marginal sales of sterling in foreign exchange markets. In fact sterling holds its value because people of many creeds and races trust us to manage our affairs with due regard to our own and their interests.

This rather awe-inspiring responsibility is an inheritance from the past. None of us here had any hand in the creation of the sterling system. It grew out of the spread of British influence during the centuries and is maintained by a complex structure of banking, insurance, shipping and international commodity markets. While the system is not controlled or consciously directed, it is held together not only by the financial and commercial structure but by the relations between the respective Governments and Monetary Authorities. If anything goes seriously wrong with the sterling system the effects will not only be felt immediately by everyone in this country but also by traders all over the world and particularly by countries whose currencies depend on sterling. The Sterling System has survived three devaluations, September 1931 (gold price 85 shillings), September 1939 (170 shillings) and September 1949 (250 shillings). All these calamities took place in special circumstances: in 1931 the great economic depression; in 1939 the outbreak of the Second War; and in 1949 when post-war political, economic and social problems were universal plagues.

We cannot look for any special set of circumstances in the world today to justify a lessening of confidence in sterling. If anything goes seriously wrong it will be entirely our own fault. If sterling were to go the way, for example, of the French franc, the consequences would not be, as is so frequently suggested, that the world would fall either in the Dollar Area or into the hands of the Bolsheviks. The immediate result would be chaos, anarchy and, unless the Gods were very kind, a collapse of civilisation as we know it over a very large area of the world. The U.S.A. could not take our place, because it has neither the banking and trading structure, the internal discipline, nor the necessary outlook. Nor could it afford to underpin the collapsed currencies of the sterling system without doing great damage to the dollar. Russia has no external monetary system—Russia's trade is financed and settled in foreign currencies, especially sterling. Communist China keeps its monetary reserves largely in sterling. You see that at any rate in the short run no one can take our place.

Sterling appears to be a very concrete thing in a weekly pay packet. In reality it is an abstraction dependent for its existence on faith in this country, its people and institutions and a belief that we will do what the world requires of us. Whether you like it or not, you have inherited the responsibilities of a great people and so far you have not let the world down.

In May 1957, he had just moved over to BOLSA and spoke at the opening of the bank's new London building. He still sounded hopeful about the use of sterling as an international currency, but outlined for the first time his view that the proper direction for Britain to look was westward, and that "European currencies and money markets will form the nucleus of a world system."

It is not perhaps a coincidence that the Bank is moving into new premises at home and is engaged in a programme of rebuilding abroad at a time when London has substantially restored its position as an international market and the use of sterling as an international currency. All that we have done is to anticipate events and put ourselves in a good position to face the future. The future of the London Market and of this Bank is, however, much more exciting than would be supposed by the casual observer looking solely at the attempt to restore the practices of the past. The fact is that the familiar political and economic structure of the world is changing very rapidly into something new and strange.

A great debate is proceeding in Europe about a Customs Union, Economic Union, a Free Trade Area, etc., attention being concentrated on the reduction of barriers which have existed in the trading field. It is not always appreciated that the Freer Trade movement will have important consequences in currency relations. The logic of the movement towards European Free Trade is the erosion of restrictions against the movement of men and money. It will be very difficult indeed to convince the citizen that it is perfectly proper and legal to buy goods from any part of Western Europe, while it remains illegal to send £10 to Aunt Agnes abroad. In the not too distant future, European currencies and money markets will form the nucleus of a world system to finance trade and capital investment.

There is, however, another important political situation which is driving Europe, including the U.K., in the direction of increasing and developing their links with the Americas, particularly Central and South America. I refer to the Suez Canal. The Canal now passes through territory in a chronic state of political anarchy. This situation has been enthusiastically promoted during recent years by certain Governments but, whatever regrets there may be about present conditions, it seems to me unlikely that much can be done about them. The Canal will certainly be used, but everyone engaged in foreign trade, foreign investment and foreign banking will consciously and subconsciously seek compensation for the insecurity which now exists by looking for more easily accessible and permanent markets.

All these changes will take place at different tempos and may appear to be spasmodic in their effect and timing, but an organisation concerned with foreign trade and foreign banking can neglect the inevitable only at its own peril. The Bank of London & South America will in future, if it is to measure up to its responsibilities, have to act as a link between the whole of Europe and Latin America.

Bolton's irrepressible pessimism, always in odd contrast with his cheerful manner and childlike smile, came into its own with the sterling crisis of 1957 and the onset of serious difficulties for the dollar. "We are returning to the horrors of peace", he said in a speech at Montreal, "with the post-war reconstruction and restocking boom over and the immediate problem posed by over-capacity and surplus raw materials rather than by inflation; with labour in an ugly mood and profit margins narrowing. But there is no need for alarm:

this is not a recession, only a new economic climate." Trade would be kept going, he believed; Europe was gaining strength and sterling was "safe for five years". But the dollar was the linch-pin of the Western World, and a dangerous situation was developing in the United States, with the drain of gold reserves, mounting foreign claims, and loss of domestic confidence. "We could not stand a weak dollar."

In the event the setback to world trade proved to be only a pause, but the next great upswing in production and prosperity was largely confined to the advanced industrial countries, while the economies mainly dependent on exporting foodstuffs and raw materials were left behind.

In the course of 1958, as the British attempt to associate with Western Europe in an industrial free trade area was defeated by the French and the six signatories of the Treaty of Rome decided to go ahead without Britain, Bolton became concerned about the early successes of the Common Market. In the Chairman's Review for 1958 he set out his own ideas for a fruitful British association with Europe.

Western Europe as a whole, including the United Kingdom, should be prepared to make a more conscious and considered contribution towards the capital development of the unsophisticated countries, more especially Latin America. In so doing, it will not only help to maintain the Western World's heritage of freedom and individual enterprise but also help itself in terms of employment, industrial activity and social stability.

It has become a matter of considerable importance that the United Kingdom should find the means of coming to terms with the members of the European Common Market. The formation of such a formidable economic bloc as the Rome Treaty envisages will certainly provide an attraction for United States investment in Europe to the detriment, as things stand at present, of the United Kingdom. A failure on our part to associate ourselves in some way with the Six could, moreover, eventually result in our being precluded from linking our surplus resources with the development of capital formation on the Continent and directing them towards the foreign investment that I have just mentioned.

If any progress is to be made during 1959 and idle productive resources put to work for the benefit of all concerned, European capital markets should be encouraged to co-ordinate their activities and mobilise the large and growing volume of savings for the purpose of increasing the total volume of foreign trade. It is to be hoped that the belated but important steps taken towards the end of 1958 to integrate European and North American currencies can be regarded as a step towards a policy which would allow European banks and financial institutions to combine their resources and expertise to finance industrialisation in Latin America and the Commonwealth.

London has the international services, financial structure, foreign banking machinery and trained man-power to enable it to play a leading part in the unification of European capital markets. And, as soon as Governments allow the European international financial system to carry out the tasks for which it was developed, many institutions in London, including this bank, will make their contribution.

These ideas were further developed in a speech at Buenos Aires in May 1959, setting out the "basic reason" for the British reluctance to take part in the European Common Market; the "tremendous responsibility" of the British people for the management of the sterling system and the general guidance of the Commonwealth.

When the war was over the U.K. had negligible reserves; tremendous debts, substantially in the form of foreign owned sterling balances; very little foreign trade; many cities devastated by bombing, and an exhausted people. The course we set was simple and not very original—it was to balance the budget, to repay our debts and restore the value and position of sterling. On this simple but sound policy we have been able to rebuild our domestic economy and foreign trade, restore the international use of sterling and the London Market and to participate in investment abroad.

There have, however, been some contributory factors which have been of assistance to the U.K. and the sterling system.

I would put high on the list the restoration of monetary discipline in Western Europe. The last example, and in many ways the most notable, is France, where for the first time for about twenty-five years paper money is being regarded with respect. But the general example of sound money behaviour is all-pervading and helps all governments to carry out what are generally regarded as unpopular policies. The consequence has been a return of capital to Western Europe, a more competitive price system and a tremendous increase in personal savings. Another important element has been the phenomenon of steadily rising prices in the U.S.A. accompanied by fears of inflation. This has aggravated the U.S. Government's difficulties in financing its vast short term debt, a problem largely of their own making and responsible for some of the fears about the dollar.

I should perhaps interpolate some comment on the European Common Market. It is not always realised that the countries included in the Common Market were organised after June 1940 by the Germans as an integrated economic and monetary unit. After the war they found themselves in various difficulties from which they were relieved by the Marshall Plan and the comprehensive organisation of Western Europe under O.E.E.C. and the European Payments Union. A continuous stimulus was therefore available over a period of fifteen years towards economic and political integration and this found its realisation in the Rome Treaty which came into force on January 1, 1959. The intentions of those responsible for the Common Market were political, using economic machinery as the vehicle for ends not clearly exposed and explained to their own people. Now, the British were not defeated or occupied in the last war: they have the temendous responsibility of the management of the Sterling System and the general guidance of the Commonwealth. It would be quite impossible to persuade the British people that their affairs should be put into the hands of a self elected and self perpetuating group in Brussels remote from Parliamentary control. This is the basic reason for the friction between Britain and the Common Market group.

Concern over the growing vulnerability of the dollar, and dissatisfaction with the lack of European co-operation in lending or investing capital overseas—these remained prominent themes throughout 1959, and they appear sharply in the Chairman's review for that year:

The maintenance of the international flow of capital is now becoming widely recognised as the most difficult problem in the political and financial field.

Two years ago, following the general fall in commodity prices, the primary producers were faced with something more radical than a temporary recession in the demand for their products. A fundamental change had probably taken place in the relative positions of the primary producers and the advanced industrial nations, with the ending of the conditions of scarcity that had prevailed since the end of the war. It is now becoming clear that we are witnessing the closing of an era. The period of post-war reconstruction is over, the lines of political division between East and West have, during the cold war, frozen solid and both sides appear willing to seek a detente based on the tacit acceptance of the status quo, while the contest between them continues. The break-up or transformation of the old colonial empires is now nearly complete, leaving much of Asia and Africa in the hands of governments whose future political evolution is doubtful and whose economic resources are weak—at least in relation to the aspirations released by independence. The recovery of Western Europe from the effects of the war has now been consolidated and its economy has acquired an independent strength, while that of the U.S.A., so long the foundation of the rest of the free world, is showing some inability to continue to carry the load of total responsibility. The problem that now faces the leading countries of the West is that of adjusting their policies to the new political and economic situations, and perhaps a greater and unwelcome responsibility falls on Europe, whose position in both relative and absolute terms has improved. Europe can and must increase its overseas investments; its economy is closely bound up with those of the primary producing nations and it remains by far the largest importing region in the world. Many of its export industries depend upon the import capacity of the less developed areas and Europe cannot afford to allow a continued fall in the purchasing power of these countries. But development plans will be hampered by inadequate capital resources and high interest costs, whether financed by international organisations or by private enterprise.

It would seem inevitable in such circumstances that if priorities and selection are not to be established, development plans should be spread over much longer periods. An alternative is for the U.S.A., Western Europe and Russia to make more resources available either by increasing taxation or by all parties substantially reducing defence expenditure to provide funds and industrial capacity for development abroad. It is perhaps too much to expect that the infantile competition between the Western World and Soviet Russia to provide certain countries supposed to be strategically important with large facilities to finance capital development should cease. The political benefits are ephemeral and, as there are in any case insufficient resources to go round, less is available for more deserving countries. Unless, therefore, some comprehensive policies are agreed among the leading Powers, the results are likely to be disappointment at home and frustration abroad.

The international status of the dollar has come under close inspection during the past year. An unfavourable balance of payments for the U.S.A. is indeed nothing new; this has been reflected in the steady growth over the past decade in foreigners' short-term claims on the U.S.A. While the dollar assets of the outside world were steadily increasing over these years, the U.S. gold stock remained comparatively stable up to the end of 1957 and not until early 1958 did foreigners begin converting their dollars into gold on any appreciable scale. There are, of course, many other factors to be taken into account in measuring the strength of the dollar:—the immense long-term assets held abroad, the U.S. drawing rights in the International Monetary Fund, and the fact that the U.S.A. accounts for about one half of the free world's economy. Nevertheless, even a country with the resources of the U.S.A. cannot accept the position of a persistent adverse balance of payments and a gold reserve protected fundamentally by abnormally high rates of interest.

For nearly two generations the U.S.A. has been able to count on a large surplus on visible trade, and increasing private claims on foreign countries, to offset most of the outgoings in respect of military aid, other government loans and grants and the overseas investments of the private sector. A most significant change in the pattern of world trade was revealed when U.S. imports, particularly of manufactured goods from Europe, were scarcely affected by the recession of 1957/58, and imports have continued to mount in 1959. How far this deterioration in the external trading position of the U.S.A. is due to ephemeral factors is a matter for argument, but even in our rapidly changing world it appears to have some element of permanency. The present situation would have appeared unthinkable when the "dollar" gap was one of the major preoccupations in Europe and it was widely held that this was a "structural" imbalance in the world economy.

Whatever qualifications may be added, it can be said of the U.S.A. in terms of the balance of payments and continually rising domestic costs, that it attempted too much even with its vast resources. The

U.S. Administration itself has seen the problem in this way, and has accepted the preservation of sound money as the most important of its tasks. Much has been done in the past year by monetary and fiscal means to reduce the strain on the economy and to equate overall demand with resources, although the problem of dealing with the public debt remains unsolved.

The development of free trade areas in Europe will no doubt attract much investment capital from the other highly industrialised countries whose manufacturers do not wish to be excluded from the benefits of participation. And there are other imponderables that will affect the flow of international investment capital: how far a general political detente may release funds for investment by lowering expenditure on armaments: the position of the U.S.S.R. either as an exporter or an importer of capital. The demands for investment at home are likely to be very large while the pressure of demand for higher standards of living in Europe will be hard to resist. Nevertheless, the annual addition to European reserves of some U.S. $1,500m. over the past decade indicates a substantial capacity for long-term foreign investment.

The industrialised countries' capacity to generate capital has increased, but the world-wide demand for capital is rising even more rapidly. Governments everywhere are committed to the maintenance of high levels of employment and the improvement of standards of living, while the world population is growing at an explosive rate. The world hunger for capital is being reflected in the level of long-term interest rates as governments, public bodies, private investors, foreign countries and international organisations bid for the limited supply. The increasing cost of the service of loans for countries whose incomes from exports have fallen tends to become a formidable proportion of their total outgoings. These considerations suggest the need for the capital-exporting centres to move towards some co-ordination of policies and, in particular, to allow their financial markets to mobilise their capital resources.

A little earlier (February, 1959) Bolton had written a private "Comment on the Foreign Exchange Situation" in which he set down some of his views on the problems of the dollar and the prospects in Europe. His remarks on the dangers of inflation even in a country as strong as the United States sound prophetic when read ten years later, when these perils have largely materialised. But this view did not lead him to look more kindly on a closer association between Britain and the European Economic Community. On the contrary, his opposition hardened.

The American economy and monetary system has been insulated from critical comment and enquiry since 1938 owing to a combination of political situations encouraging a massive movement of capital to the U.S.A. and a persistently favourable balance of payments. During the last twenty years the dollar has become the unchallenged measure and store of value of the Western World and, in consequence, central banks have tended to treat the dollar as being as good as, if not better than, gold. This situation is illustrated in the operation of the International Monetary Fund, the International Bank for Reconstruction & Development and the European Payments Union, and similar institutions where the monetary standard is, and most transactions have been made in, the dollar. Until recently it has been the habit of most, although not all, central banks to hold a substantial proportion of reserves in dollars, which has meant that the U.S. Government was, and is, being financed by foreign central banks to the extent that their monetary reserves are invested in U.S. Treasury bills.

Two devastating world wars were the main reasons for the growth of American financial power, which grew as Europe wrecked itself politically and destroyed its accumulated wealth. European domestic currencies weakened to the extent that capital formation became a game of hide-and-seek between authority seeking to mobilise savings for national purposes and individuals trying to export and hide savings abroad, especially in the U.S.A. The U.S.A. benefited in two ways: they had the incentive to expand and produce—untrammelled by monetary or political anxieties—and domestic savings were reinforced by foreign Governments, central banks and private foreign investors. The economic and monetary situation of the U.S.A. in the '40s and '50s, while established on the foundation of American wealth and natural resources, was also very solidly underpinned by the international political situation. The U.S.A. has, in consequence, been lulled into a frame of mind in which the experience of the last twenty years is regarded as the natural consequence of innate American superiority in industrial production, political philosophy and monetary management.

Accidents of history have played a larger part in the process than is generally accepted, and the effect of accidents wears off.

It is thirteen years since the end of the second world war, and industry in the Western World has been restored and modernised; consumer demand is largely satisfied; sophisticated countries' domestic demand for capital goods is diminishing; and surpluses of raw materials are re-emerging. But the most important change is in military tactics and strategy, following developments in weapons of mass destruction through the agency ultimately of long-range rockets. These foreshadow the end of the citizen army and conscription and in some countries orthodox forces are already being cut down substantially. In all countries Government orders for aeroplanes, anti-aircraft weapons, heavy surface vessels, etc., are being reduced. Admittedly, the new weapons are hideously expensive, but they employ relatively small numbers of men in manufacture and military use, and traditional military raw materials are used only to a minimal extent.

We therefore have at least two important factors at work combining to reduce (a) the demand for raw materials, (b) employment in all countries, and (c) the volume and value of foreign trade. Some of the consequences of these major changes in the international economic climate have been felt in the much publicised "recession" in the U.S.A., a minor manifestation of a more deep-seated disturbance.

In spite of the continued friction between our world and the Communist bloc, it is not impossible that we have reached one of those periods, which frequently occur in history, of uneasy political and military balance. The major antagonists have used up most of their ideas, a new generation is emerging and the conflict tends to die down out of boredom and the human need for change. In any event, mutual extinction is a powerful deterrent to the acceptance of war as a normal part of national policy. Economic factors may therefore play a greater part than in times of hot and cold war, when all policies appear to be governed by a simple military objective. We may be facing a long period of transition, and the country facing a larger crop of problems than any other is the U.S.A.

Owing to the circumstances previously described, Washington has rarely felt the need to observe the timid precepts that have tended elsewhere to govern orthodox budget practice and the management of government debt. The budget is in substantial deficit; 80 per cent of government debt is short-term and a large proportion matures in 1959. The U.S.A. is no longer regarded as the only home for foreign capital, nor is the dollar as good as gold. Substantial amounts of gold have been lost to the U.S. reserves since 1957, with no perceptible reduction in foreign claims on the U.S. banking system.

The underlying foreign trade and economic situation has already produced unemployment at a time when all democratic governments, including the United States Government, are committed to take measures to prevent the growth of unemployment. The measures already undertaken by Washington, rightly or wrongly, induce some feeling in the U.S.A. that inflation is inevitable and there has been a movement out of fixed interest securities and savings into equities. The measures taken have already produced some disturbance in the foreign exchanges: it is evident that if these measures are inadequate in relation to a full employment policy, and Washington were to decide to use techniques of a more extreme nature, the dollar might be in danger. On the other hand, if the Administration were to regard the stability of the dollar as having first priority, they would have little option but to reduce budget deficits and prevent credit inflation. Looking back, it is difficult to avoid the impression that American foreign policy was essentially one of unlimited liability. The financial burden of this, particular in times of emergency, fell upon the American tax-payer and the apparently unlimited resources of the U.S.A. But once the dollar becomes exposed to some of the hazards that have disturbed weaker currencies, then foreign policy may become affected by unexpected restraints.

Any modern State, especially the U.S.A., depends for its survival and growth on the ability to create debt and the willingness of the private individual and banks and corporations to invest in debt. But once money becomes suspect, this essential element in the economic organisation begins to break down and governments become incapable of managing their monetary affairs, and eventually of governing the country. I hold the view that the value and standing of paper money is of greater importance than any other single factor in the make-up of the modern State. It can be given second place only when a country is in mortal danger, as the U.K. was during 1939/41, when everything was thrown into the balance in the determination to survive. But in peace time, however qualified the phrase, money comes first. Any other policy is bound to fail because the people cannot be deceived for any length of time beyond their first real experience of declining money. Many European countries have had their unfortunate experiences of paper money with diminishing, if not vanishing, value. It is difficult—and it is going to be even more difficult in the future—to deceive the average American and Briton, and persuade them to accept payment for wages and to put their long-term trust in money which they know to be declining in value. The general monetary and budgetary policy of the United States Administration is therefore likely to have considerable repercussions over a wide field, and I would hope that the easy path for temporary political gain is avoided.

Recent events in Europe may also have some effect on the relative power and importance of the U.S. dollar. The decision by the British monetary authorities to unify transferable, American and Canadian account sterling under the name of "external sterling" produces, for the first time since the beginning of the war, a situation where the respective positions of the dollar and sterling systems can be expressed through a single rate of exchange. This decision, however, was only a part of the comprehensive move towards convertibility undertaken by practically all the European governments at the turn of the year. As a result, all the Western European currencies and the dollar are now interchangeable in terms of foreign trade and finance. The change reveals, for the first time, the growing economic and financial power of Western Europe, including in this description the sterling system. Much depends upon the success of the measures introduced by the new French government. So far, there is no doubt whatsoever of the first impact of these measures, which have brought about a considerable reflux of gold and foreign exchange into the Bank of France. It is also true that the confidence of the French people, both in their currency and in their Government, has immeasurably improved, and there are good grounds for believing that this improvement will continue. If some means can be found to reduce the monetary haemorrhage caused by the conflict in Algeria, one could be quite certain that there would be a massive influx of capital into France. The effect of such a movement would be felt by all countries, but to the greatest extent by Switzerland and the U.S.A.

The present conflict between the countries included in the Common Market under the Rome Treaty, and the rest of Europe including the

United Kingdom, may postpone the unification, which I believe to be inevitable, of European capital markets. The real issue is not over trade discrimination, although this is, of course, of very great importance, but over the difference between the political objectives of the Common Market countries and the rest of Europe. It is not generally realised that the Rome Treaty introduces comprehensive supra-national policies and the protagonists hope ultimately to achieve by this method the political unification of the six countries. However, if the United Kingdom were acceptable as a member, and this is uncertain, it is extremely doubtful whether the British public, as a whole, is at all ready to consider the gradual handing over of the monetary and economic structure into the hands of groups over whom it would have at the most an indirect influence. I therefore regretfully come to the conclusion that it is going to be execessively difficult for the United Kingdom and the British Commonwealth to organise satisfactory trade relations with the Common Market. This, however, should not exclude the possibility of closer financial links between the sterling system and the Common Market countries, particularly as the first step, namely convertibility, has already been taken.

In 1960 the pressure on the dollar duly reached a climax, with widespread loss of confidence and a speculative run on gold which led, by the autumn, to a steep rise in the market price of gold. Emergency measures were taken in Washington to relieve the tension. Bolton was concerned that Europe seemed unprepared to take some of the weight off America's shoulders and pleaded again for greater capital exports from Western Europe to the less developed countries, particularly to Latin America. The following passages, taken from his review of events in 1960, illustrate his constant personal efforts to see the world as a whole.

The acquisition of greater economic and financial power by Europe has not occurred uniformly and, although it would be an exaggeration to say that the United Kingdom has not shared in this growth, it remains true that the expansion of production and trade has been more pronounced in the continental countries, particularly in Germany. Moreover, although in trade matters the Six have evolved a certain unity of purpose, it cannot be said that there is any significant coordination of basic economic policies. Each country continues to be largely preoccupied with its own domestic problems and they have so far given little thought to the pooling of both problems and resources in such a way as to lead to the emergence of Europe as a unified economic power.

It seems clear that only a Europe in which there is a real co-ordination of financial resources and economic thinking—something more permanent and far-reaching than the unification of Customs tariffs—can effectively accept and develop an unavoidable share of the responsibility for assisting the under-capitalised countries of the western world. A year ago I remarked that the United States economy was showing some inability to continue to carry the load of total responsibility for the under-developed territories; the events of 1960 have confirmed this, but the European countries are slow in realising their potential strength in this sphere.

Among the reasons for this slowness is the persistence of monetary and fiscal regulations that tend to restrict expansion beyond purely domestic needs and, by perpetuating the problems associated with economic crisis and austerity, prevent any international policy co-ordination, and impede the free movement of people and resources. Also, the continued and rising level of military expenditure in some countries, with the accompanying high level of taxation, is to some extent responsible for the fear of inflation that prompts the retention of restrictive measures. It is an unfortunate fact that, where governments absorb a large proportion of the money supply for unproductive and inflationary expenditure, it is necessary to restrict the growth of credit in the private sector. A significant lowering of the intensity of the cold war—which may depend largely on Mr. Kennedy and his advisers—could lead to a reduction in defence expenditure by the western countries and the abolition of exchange controls, and might enable the European financial centres to mobilise their substantial capital resources for use in overseas development.

Another factor of some importance—again reflecting the self-centred nature of most European thinking—has been the purely commercial view taken by the developed countries of the under-developed. This is noticeable in Latin America which is commonly regarded, both in continental Europe and in the United Kingdom, as an area of trade opportunities rather than as a group of twenty republics with particular social and economic problems. This is not to say that no financial assistance has been given: lengthening credit terms have been demanded by Latin American buyers and given by the more enterprising exporters, in many cases with their governments' support; and there have been substantial investments of industrial capital; but the idea of a deliberate campaign designed to provide aid for basic development has received no attention.

The growth of this idea may have been retarded by the feeling that, for the reasons I have suggested, none of the European economies—with the possible exception of the German—is sufficiently strong alone to give a volume of direct aid significant enough to contribute materially to the large social problems of Latin America. It may be taken as indicative of the absence of the concept of Europe as a financial unit that there is no mechanism in existence, other than purely temporary arrangements among private banks, whereby the financial resources of the European countries, however limited individually, could be developed and channelled into the emergent economies where they are needed. The United Kingdom, for example, has given substantial aid to Commonwealth and ex-colonial territories, but the sense of responsibility does not extend to Latin America and we have no policy based upon financial association with European markets.

It is doubtful whether the purely commercial assistance that Europe is giving to the under-capitalised countries—particularly in Latin America—is enough to meet the urgent problems that are arising. The population growth in the whole of Latin America is in the order of two-and-a-half per cent annually, and in certain regions it is higher. To prevent an actual fall in per capita incomes, national incomes must be increased at a greater pace, an effort at present beyond the capacity of countries that are still essentially producers and exporters of primary commodities.

The larger and more advanced republics have been engaged for some twenty years in building up industries as a means of raising productivity and the incomes of at least some sectors of their populations. This has resulted in the now familiar changes in the composition of their imports, with the emphasis on capital goods and raw materials; this in turn has led to changes in methods of payment. The classical "bill on London" was a useful means of financing the exchange of consumer goods that were for immediate re-sale in the country of destination, but the system is no longer adequate for equipment that cannot earn its cost over less than five or ten years.

Beyond these immediate commercial considerations lies the broader concept of the twenty Latin American republics as members of the Western World, towards whom the developed countries may be said to have certain obligations. It is not difficult to think of instances where an apparent failure on the part of, for instance, the U.S.A. to appreciate and fulfil such obligations has been the cause of antagonism. Cuba is a good example of the neglect of the social consequences of fostering exclusive relations with the business and wealthy classes.

An international programme is urgently required to:

1. restore the stability of the pattern of exchanges;
2. end the unhealthy concentration on gold, both as a private store of value and as a commodity likely to increase in price; it is useless to expect the international exchanges to carry out their main task of providing the channel for trade and finance if the medium of ultimate settlement, viz. gold, is subject to continuous speculation.
3. remove the restrictions which keep European capital markets apart and thus allow the growing volume of savings to be made available to finance the capital needs of countries that are engaged in developing their industrial capacity.

LATIN AMERICAN VISION

A visit to Paris, to attend the opening of BOLSA's new premises, gave an opportunity to plead for greater financial and commercial interest in Latin America. After pointing out that the bank had existed for nearly one hundred years and had maintained a branch in Paris for longer than any other British Bank, Bolton went on to say that since the end of the second world war, European interest in Latin America had quickened:

Not only France but other countries in Europe, from both sides of the iron curtain, are all exerting greater efforts to increase both their trade with, and their investment in, Latin America. The reason is not far to seek: countries of Western Europe have seen their political and economic empires and other spheres of influence in the Near, Middle and Far East eroded by major changes in the international political climate, and by the blandishments of offers of economic assistance from sources untrammelled by obligations established by the experience of generations of social and political maturity. The areas of the world where the western nations can still trade on purely commercial terms without being suspected of some hidden political motive are rapidly diminishing, and it is not surprising therefore that in recent years Western Europe has been turning its eyes to the Western Hemisphere, and especially to Latin America, where the possibilities of economic and social development are almost unlimited; where the marriage of Europe's technical experience and great industrial capacity with the natural resources of that continent and the enthusiastic aspirations of its peoples hold the promise of a brilliant future for both parties.

> As Chairman of BOLSA he had many opportunities to study the economic problems of Latin America, and the urgent needs of the region impressed him increasingly. He saw clearly its dependence on a large, sustained flow of foreign investment capital; and he was well aware that this flow was being restrained not only by European indifference but by monetary instability in most Latin American countries. His views at that time were developed in an article written for "The Statist" in 1960.

Too little attention has perhaps been given to the profoundly disturbing effect on the economic development of the Latin American republics of the decline and persistent weakness of primary commodity prices. The South American group, with the possible exception of Venezuela, has felt the impact of this trend with some severity.

Development and industrialisation are aspects of a process which acquires a pace of its own that is hard to change, particularly to moderate once it has gained excessive speed. The South American countries, of which Argentina and Brazil are prominent examples, have experienced virtually all the vicissitudes of shortages of goods, of high-cost industries, of dwindling export earnings and intractable inflation, and of the shortage of development capital. The pressing need to maintain imports at a certain and mounting level so as to avoid industrial recession with its bankruptcies and unemployment has, in conjunction with entirely inelastic export earnings, made it necessary to finance a part of these imports with loans from abroad, often from the suppliers.

Since the end of the second world war the principal source of industrial credit and development loans has been the U.S.A. and the international organisations that have their headquarters in that country; Europe in the last fifteen years has been recovering its own prosperity and has taken only a minor part in financing economic progress in South America. The emergence of Europe as an important source of development capital, and the realisation that the payments deficit of the U.S.A. is more than a temporary reversal of the familiar trend, are factors in the international scene that the South Americans are now, belatedly perhaps, beginning to appreciate.

The implication that should be faced in the United Kingdom is that the South American republics will be looking more towards Europe than they have done in the past: they will be readier to consider offers of supplies and of financial assistance from Europe, and less obsessed with the importance of the dollar. This is obviously true of Argentina and Brazil, but will also be found to apply in different degrees to the west coast countries, Chile and Peru, and even to some extent in Colombia.

In these circumstances, which are so favourable to Europe as a whole, the United Kingdom may take or lose an opportunity to participate in the economic development of Latin America: there can be little doubt that if it is lost, the opportunity will not recur: the other European countries will leave no room for late comers.

Progress now being made by the Latin American nations towards a free trade area, and ultimately a common market or even an economic community, is an indication that eventually, when these aims become a working reality, investments in the area will be investments in a large and rapidly expanding sector of the world's economy. Investors and traders may be excused, though not always justified, for having doubts and hesitations about individual Latin American countries, but the monetary discipline required to made the free trade area work—as eventually it will—will be a guarantee of reasonable stability in general.

> Repeated visits to Latin America deepened his interest. Like many other travellers in that continent he was impressed with its enormous scope for economic and social development, and he was perplexed by the practical difficulties of attracting sufficient foreign capital to the area. Speaking about "Latin America in the sixties" to a conference of the Advertising Association in 1960, he outlined some of these problems.

Though my subject is Latin America in the sixties, it is not altogether out of place to recall that one hundred years ago saw the awakening interest of British businessmen in the potentialities of Latin America as a field of trade and investment. The year 1862 saw the foundation both of the institution that was later to become the Bank of London and South America and of the first major British railway enterprise in that continent. I am told that the first manager of the London & River Plate Bank landed in Buenos Aires with two boxes, one containing his clothes and the other, bags of sovereigns. He at once started banking business in a fishing hut just beyond the high tide mark. From these beginnings there developed a flood of British investment in Latin America—in Argentina above all, but to some extent in all the other major republics—that reached full tide in the decade before the First World War. Towards the end of this period, investments from France, Germany and other European countries, as well as from the U.S.A., were growing in importance, but the British role as provider of capital was predominant and served to reinforce the trading position of this country as the leading exporter of Europe which, as a whole, sold well over twice as much as the U.S.A. to Latin America. The British contribution to financing the first great period of economic expansion in modern Latin America in the latter half of the nineteenth century and beginning of the twentieth was comparable to its role in building up the leading territories of our own Empire. On the eve of the first world war investments in Latin America approached one quarter of all British overseas investments.

Britain's relations with the rest of the world have undergone profound changes since those days, but in no other major region of the world has there been such a decline of British trade, investment, and influence. Two world wars and the temporary shift of economic power from Europe to the U.S.A. were largely responsible for the change. In the inter-war years the U.S.A. supplanted Europe as the main supplier of development capital to Latin America. Britain's stake in Latin America remained very large, and that region continued to supply—as it still does—an important part of our requirements of foodstuffs and raw materials, but United Kingdom trade with Latin America never regained its pre-1914 volume. Moreover, as economic development was itself changing the nature of the continent's imports, Britain's competitors in the twenties and thirties were more successful in adapting themselves to the changing needs of their Latin American customers. During and immediately after the second world war, with the scaling down of official debts and the repatriation of capital investment in railways and other utilities, there was a large-scale liquidation of British and other European investments in Latin America, and the position of the U.S.A. in both investment and trade became predominant. The Monroe Doctrine was expanded into the Pan-American Movement, the Association of American States, and was accompanied by charges of Yankee Imperialism. It is no coincidence that the U.S.A. became the dominant trading and political partner of Latin America during the same period that it became the major source of capital; and it is clear that the connection between trade, politics and capital movements, always close, will remain a vital factor in determining the pattern of Latin America's import trade in the next ten years.

We now stand at the watershed between two eras in the financial and economic—and perhaps also in the political—history of the post-war world, and this is a most opportune time for reconsidering the nature of our economic relationship to the major groups of countries overseas. We have already been faced with a fundamental re-appraisal of our relationship with the Empire—now the Commonwealth—and with Europe, and our attitude towards Latin Amercia must be included in this reconsideration of the world we live in. Our preoccupation with the Commonwealth stands out as an obvious partial explanation for the comparative neglect of Latin America in the post-war years. It is natural that British businessmen should have preferred the well-known and comparatively safe markets and investment opportunities of the Commonwealth, well provided with sterling; in contrast to those markets the complexities and uncertainties of Latin America appeared doubly discouraging. In addition there were the adverse psychological effects of the large-scale liquidation of British interests in Latin America immediately after the war and the discouragements afforded by such experiences as the Brazilian default on its commerical obligations in the early 1950's. Some old-established connections with Latin America still remain; many exporters continue to carry on a profitable business with Latin America and a few significant investments have been made since the war. But the general effect of the combination of post-war problems caused the United Kingdom to neglect its old connections and in reality to forget the existence of Latin America.

More recently there have been some signs of greater interest, both private and official, with, for example Royal and official visits and the re-opening of B.O.A.C.'s South American route, but practical enthusiasm is lacking. As you are all aware, little attention is given to Latin America by the press of the U.K. The image of Latin America that persists in the public mind is unflattering; there is no clear picture of a region of twenty separate republics, differing widely in character, political maturity and economic development. Undue concentration on sensational events, such as revolutions—generally bloodless—has tended to obscure the fact that most of the republics of Latin America have made notable progress towards political stability and more democratic government over the past decade. Moreover, the political uncertainties in a number of countries in the post-war years have had no lasting effect on economic development, which, while following a course influenced by government actions, has been substantially independent of the superficial excitements of politics.

Nor have conditions in Latin America since the war discouraged a massive investment of private and official United States capital. To this there has been added in the second half of the fifties a growing influx of European capital. This has been particularly the case in Brazilian industry where the German investment has been especially notable. The Latin American republics are by no means unwilling to look more readily to Europe as a source of capital and to lessen their dependance on the "colossus of the North". This is more especially the case now that the dollar no longer enjoys the prestige of the early post-war years.

Just as the closing of the fifties has brought to an end the era of post-war reconstruction in Europe and the restoration to that continent of its independent strength, so for Latin America too an era has ended, though with less favourable consequences. Latin America enjoyed for more than a decade after the end of the war a period of rising prosperity and rapid economic growth that was to a large extent based on two factors; firstly, the use of accumulated wartime earnings of foreign exchange, which were soon exhausted and secondly, on very favourable terms of trade which, as the ending of post-war scarcities has brought about a general fall in commodity prices, are now reversed. During these years the larger republics pushed ahead with industrialisation plans and with the extension of roads, power supplies and the rest of the economic infrastructure.

Industrialisation and the general economic expansion that is necessary if the countries of Latin America are to meet the needs of their rapidly growing populations can, however, only be sustained with external assistance. With the depletion of these countries' reserves of gold and foreign exchange and with the fall in the prices of their exports and hence of their earnings of foreign currencies, they have become increasingly dependent on foreign capital to sustain economic development. This capital is being sought in the form of trade credit, long-term official loans and direct investment in industry. Most of Latin America is looking for fresh sources of capital and is likely to look increasingly to Europe. The combined countries of the European Economic Community dispose of a rapidly growing commercial and economic power and the major industrial and financial institutions in these countries may be expected to act increasingly in concert as exporters of capital. Fears that the capital generated within the Community will be wholly absorbed by the Community itself and in its associated overseas territories are exaggerated. Latin Amercia can certainly provide investment opportunities of a kind for which the dependent or formerly-dependent territories of Africa will not be ready for many years to come.

The U.K., as a country whose prosperity is largely dependent on foreign trade and the international services it provides, cannot afford to neglect any opportunity for expanding its overseas interests. The whole of Latin America does not appear a large market in a total U.K. export of nearly £3,500 million a year, nevertheless it is a region on which this country depends for a number of vital imports. Last year this country purchased over £320 million worth of Latin American goods, or more than twice as much as it exported there. The present time is one of economic difficulties for many of the Latin American republics, but they remain countries with an enormous potential for growth. They are reckoned under-developed, or even poor, by Western European standards, but poverty is a relative term. The major republics are rich in natural resources; they have already made good economic progress and have reached a stage of development and income per head of population that is far ahead of most of Asia and Africa. There is not in Latin America the same pressure of numbers upon living space and resources that makes the problem of raising living standards in Asia very nearly insoluble. The political and economic future of much of Asia and Africa is uncertain. But Latin America, it cannot be too often stressed, is, by history, culture and conviction, an integral part of the Western World.

By 1975, the population of Latin America will have increased from 200,000,000 to 300,000,000 and vast areas of empty land will have been developed. There are no serious political conflicts likely to lead to the arbitrament of war and, in fact, Latin American political behaviour during the twentieth century compares very favourably with the destruction and descent to savagery so characteristic of much of Europe in the same period.

> He went on developing this theme—that Europe, including Britain, should take a more active interest in Latin American affairs—in a long series of speeches and articles, wherever he could find someone to listen or read. Typical is a speech to a group of British manufacturers in May, 1961.

During the nineteenth century, the Monroe Doctrine—which few realise was the creation of Canning, our great Foreign Secretary—isolated the emergent republics of Latin America from European political influence. Brazil retained its Portuguese background, and the Royal Family, the Braganzas, provided Emperors for Brazil until 1889, having first been taken to Brazil by the British Navy in order to avoid capture by the French. Under the cloak of the Monroe Doctrine and the Royal Navy, South America was largely developed by British capital, which provided the finance for most of the railways, ports, gas works, municipal developments (such as water, sewage, roads and transport), domestic trading companies and banks—of which the Bank of London & South America is today the only remaining British bank.

The first world war brought this phase to an end, and the United States began to overtake Britain as the main source of the capital needed by South America. The second world war brought about the wholesale liquidation of British investment in South America, to provide for the war effort.

The United States virtually "took over" financially and became the principal suppliers of the capital equipment and consumer goods which could not be produced locally. Politically, Latin America became an American preserve—under the "Good Neighbour Policy"—and it was assumed in Washington that their southern neighbours were to be guided and aided mainly by the U.S.A., to whom their due gratitude and loyalty would be given.

This was, of course, a gross over-simplification of a very complicated situation. Northern American influence never became as completely predominant as that, for the Latin American republics have always been sturdy upholders of their hard-won independence. Nevertheless, the time has now come when the predominance of the United States is no longer taken for granted. Cuba marks the end of a phase, and it is clear that the various Latin American countries intend to seek their own ways of emerging from their dependence on the more highly industrialised countries of the West. Each country has its own individual economic and social problems and is pursuing its own political policies. But there is already a tendency for some of the traditional barriers between the republics to break down. The concept of Latin America is beginning to acquire social and political meaning.

It is well known that Latin America is one of the few major areas of the world still thinly populated. It is also common knowledge that the population of the area is increasing rapidly. The current population is two hundred million; by 1975 it will be three hundred million; and by the end of the century six hundred million. These figures do not really mean very much, however, for in the twenty independent republics there are geographical, climatic, soil and ethnic differences that make most generalisations misleading. There is, however, one important common factor. They are all European in their social, legal and cultural inheritance, and there are no "colour" questions.

The policies being followed today by the Latin American republics are aimed at overcoming the position of economic inferiority into which they have been forced by constantly worsening terms of trade. Their first thought, therefore, has been, for many years, industrialisation. By building up industrial communities, it has been possible for Latin American governments to achieve three things. First, there has been a rise in the living standards of at least certain sectors of the population, although there is little evidence that these benefits have penetrated to the semi-destitute peasant communities. On the contrary, the contrasts between living conditions of the urban and rural dwellers have been—in many cases—accentuated. Second, a certain measure of self-sufficiency in many industrial products has been achieved, generally by means of highly protectionist policies. Third, it has been possible to attract foreign industrial capital, frequently by giving a quasi-monopoly to the foreign owned subsidiary.

The effect of this trend towards a rather artificially stimulated industrial growth has been—in the more advanced countries such as Argentina and Brazil—the exclusion of many products that were formerly imported. Manufacturers in Europe and the U.S.A., who once had good markets in the countries that are now industrialising rapidly, often find that the only way to retain or regain a share of such markets is to establish a local manufacturing subsidiary.

In considering the Latin American countries as markets for British goods, or for British capital and skill in the production of goods locally, the questions that first arise are those concerning any country's economic management, its growth potential, its capacity for overseas payments, and so forth. Equally important—though less frequently recognised—are the social problems and the interplay of political forces that goes on below the surface.

Concurrently with the industrial revolution that is taking place in Latin America (with Argentina, Brazil and Mexico in the lead) is the social and political revolutionary trend that is slowly changing these countries from oligarchies into democracies in the economic sense. The republics that were born some one hundred and fifty years ago inherited from Iberian rule a system of land tenure—and therefore of wealth—that resulted in a few immensely rich families being in control of a country's politics, finances, production and general progress. The landless peasants and workers received no larger share of the national income than the ruling families cared to allow. Many rural communities living on unproductive land, the higher slopes of the Andes and North Eastern Brazil, are still seriously under-nourished, lacking in basic education and medical care, and unable to improve their lot in their native surroundings unaided. These were the facts underlying the social revolution in Bolivia in 1952, and the more recent events in Cuba. They explain the widespread support that Castro receives wherever such conditions exist today.

I would say, therefore, that the developed nations of the Western World should consider the need to aid the Latin American countries —which are a large and essential part of the West—to develop into integrated economic democracies. Unless, in fact, we in Europe are willing to devote to such a case a larger proportion of our relatively abundant wealth, we run the risk of failing to prevent or at least help to prevent, a series of upheavals that might further and dangerously reduce the potential of the Western World.

Apart from the actions that are required of governments and central banks in this sense, industrialists and investors can contribute by channelling resources and skill into Latin American manufacturing industries. It is no longer possible to think of the Latin American republics as so many markets with cash to spend on a given volume of goods. They are peoples that need our help in developing into nations that can be our trading partners in the same way that European countries are partners among themselves.

In the course of this campaign he spoke a good deal to meetings of students—usually with a view to attracting one or two promising young men to a career with BOLSA. For example, speaking to the "Magnates Club" at Oxford, he drew a colourful picture of the opportunities awaiting the intelligent, well-trained graduate in various professional and business careers in Latin America. This work continued over the years and brought useful results.

On an extended visit to Latin America during 1961 he made a number of speeches pointing to the recovery of Western Europe and the need to stimulate European capital exports. The following extracts from a speech in Buenos Aires set the theme.

Since I was here last, the growth of the economic and monetary strength of the countries of Western Europe has continued. This rapid acquisition of financial power has necessarily been at the expense of the United States, and there has been a significant change in the distribution of capital wealth and resources on both sides of the Atlantic. But the distribution of political responsibility remains unchanged, and most countries, especially in Latin America, continue to look to Washington for capital. This economic development to Western Europe has, however, been at times a hazardous process as, by its sheer rapidity, it has brought tensions in the exchanges accompanied by speculative and, at times, massive movements of money with the consequences you see today. The flow of money into Germany and the consequent pressure on the dollar—which came to a head last October with the steep rise in the price of gold on the London market—was the major event of 1960. The German and Dutch revaluations in February 1961 set off fresh waves of anxiety and speculation based on the possibility of more revaluation. One immediate result was the massive flow of hot money to Switzerland, accompanied by an attack on sterling. The prospect of periodic eruptions in the international exchanges encourages capital to take advantage of the speculative conditions that are offered from time to time, and this can only be to the detriment of banking credit for commerce and of capital available for longer term investment.

The immediate sufferers in these conditions are those countries with urgent needs for development capital, but in the longer run the inevitable result of continued turbulence in the exchanges must be a contraction of world trade.

The steps taken by the European central banks have had a stabilising effect on the international exchanges. I regard this move towards a co-ordinated exchange policy as one of the greatest importance, as I consider it vital to the prosperity of the Western World that order be returned to the international exchange markets.

As you know, the British Government is now committed to examining the pros and cons of Common Market membership. Apart from the importance of the Commonwealth link there are other major political decisions involved, such as relations with Russia and the economic consequences to Latin America. I feel that discrimination against Latin American production might have unfortunate consequences.

There is still no effective machinery to co-ordinate the financial resources of Europe, so that it can undertake its full share of responsibility in assisting the undercapitalised countries of the Western World. There is, however, a growing recognition in Europe that the countries that have made rapid economic progress, and have acquired considerable reserves, e.g., Germany and Italy, should assume a greater share of the responsibility for the growth of the less developed countries, and should return their surplus funds into international circulation in the form of economic aid, development credits and so on. European countries have been slow to adopt any co-ordinated policy of capital re-export, principally I believe because after so many years of reconstruction and the ever present fear of inflation they have been unable to recognise prosperity for what it is.

The complaint that "England has forgotten Latin America" led Bolton to a sharp criticism of British government policies. In an interview with "Vision" in 1962 he replied to the question:

"*Does the British Government do enough to encourage investors to enlarge their operations in Latin America?*"

No. There is a lot of talk, but very little is actually done. Exhortations are not enough to make exporters interested in a market where financing is difficult and the credit standing of customers is low. The policy of the British Government in the matter of loans discriminates in favour of the Commonwealth.

I believe that the financing of Latin America should be restored, since we shall otherwise lose the cold war. There are two hundred million people in Latin America. Before long the population will have risen to three hundred million. Imagine the consequences if they should fall under Communist control. What is the sense in worrying about the number of troops in NATO when there is this possibility in Latin America?

The restoration of the financing of Latin America should be done by stages. It should begin with an international rescue operation in which the U.S.A. would play the leading part and Europe would give decisive co-operation.

Europe should organise something similar to the Export-Import Bank or should establish some other machinery whereby governments can guarantee loans that are granted. This should be done not on a national, but on an international basis.

"*Is there any likelihood that Britain or the European Common Market will initiate their own aid programme for Latin America?*"

They ought to initiate such programmes, for political reasons. If business declines in Europe, which is not at all improbable, industrialists will begin to look for new markers, always provided that they can find means of financing them. But it is not to be expected that Europe could do much in Latin America in this respect. The fact is that there is not enough capital in the world to meet the needs of the underdeveloped countries. Each of those countries has been led to believe, however, that there is enough.

"*Are you therefore pessimistic about the prospects in Latin America?*"

The Bank of London & South America is not at all pessimistic. It is at present engaged in an enormous building programme in Latin America, in spite of the difficulties that it has had to face hitherto and those that will doubtless appear in the future. But we are doing this because we believe that it is one of the most interesting and most important parts of the world. Latin America will survive. It ought, however, to modify its aims and objectives. Latin America will not attain the same living standards as the U.S.A. in only ten years. The future should be planned in terms of fifty or a hundred years, not five of ten.

> Latin America remained in the centre of his eye throughout the years that followed, and his faith in the future of this region grew stronger even while he grappled with the bewildering political and economic problems which waxed and waned. By 1969, seven years after the confident predictions just quoted, his hope had become conviction. He saw Latin America well on the way to taking a leading place in the Western World, rivalling Europe in economic strength and surpassing her in political maturity. The following review, published early in 1969, shows how his enthusiasm crystallised as he came to know more of Latin American history and current problems.

Latin America must be included in any international economic and political survey made today. It is foreseeable that by the end of the century this comparatively unknown and neglected group of countries will have acquired a political weight and economic strength that Europe, apparently condemned to continuing fragmentation along ethnic lines, will come to envy. It is pertinent in this connection that Latin America is the only region in the world inhabited by people of varied ethnic origins that is not significantly affected by racial disharmony; the value of this asset will be truly appreciated only in the coming decades when multiple tragedies may afflict other continents. The future of Latin America must inevitably appear very much more assured than that of Africa, which now seems doomed to be riven into ever more numerous fractions through divisions along racial, religious and tribal lines.

The Latin Americans may seem at present to be rather unsure of their role, but their evolution has been rapid and some of the republics are undoubtedly destined to become world leaders. It may not be very obvious to the politicians and economists of the rich nations that what they have called the "developing world" includes countries at opposite ends, as well as in the middle, of the scale of economic and social advancement. Several of the Latin American republics are at the top of the scale and are becoming eligible for a change of status; by the end of this century the term "Latin America" will mean something as clearly defined and as significant as the E.E.C. or COMECON, and probably as influential economically as either. The South American states will of necessity pursue and widen the scope of their relations with countries in other continents—countries that for different reasons will be ready to co-operate. Across the Pacific, for example, there are already many technical connections with Japan and agricultural exchanges with Australia and New Zealand; and there is considerable academic and technical interest in China as a source of new ideas.

This trend is likely to be accentuated as the cost of the U.S. involvement in Vietnam inevitably leads the new Administration in Washington to rethink its policies towards Latin America, where, in any case, the concept of "hemisphere solidarity" has in many aspects proved unpalatable to the Latin Americans. In fact, the dislike and fear of foreign economic penetration, particularly from North America, probably lies at the root of the current, doubtless transient, manifestations of xenophobia. These are not peculiar to the Latin American countries, as is illustrated by the case of Canada, and are due to an understandable fear of the sheer size of American corporations and a belief that they carry out Washington foreign policy with little regard to local interests.

The U.S. Administration, nevertheless, advised by the Pentagon, may well continue to regard Latin America as an area of direct strategic importance and may continue to believe that it is possible to dictate military and economic policy to the Latin American countries for strategic reasons. Such an approach is unlikely to succeed for long and will have diminishing relevance for a region that, before the end of the century, will have acquired its own international status and will have its own military and commercial agreements all over the world. There is more than enough capacity and determination in the continent for the Latin Americans successfully to face the challenge of a cessation of aid and perhaps investment from the U.S.A., and to accept with equanimity the abandonment in Europe of all pretence at trade liberalisation. It would not be surprising if, in such circumstances, and long before 1999, the economic growth-rate of Latin America were to exceed that of an increasingly restricted Europe.

In common with other parts of the world, the Latin Americans have discovered that the principles of orthodox monetary management are in more or less constant conflict with the urgent need for social and economic change and especially for constitutional reform. The more advanced nations of Latin America have by now acquired enough experience of inflationary government policies to know that too much zeal for change can too easily lead to over-expenditure, and that instant reform of four hundred-year-old structures is not always feasible. They have found that it is impossible for even the most ambitious and skilful government to achieve reforms at the speed demanded by the political idealists, and that if it is attempted it can only be at the price of rapid inflation. Besides the monetary effects of budget deficits, a sudden redistribution of income implies a transfer of purchasing power to a large number of new consumers and is likely to have inflationary consequences, however carefully handled. It is largely because of the urgency of their social problems and the eruption of strong feelings over the consequences of these conflicting economic principles that the Latin Americans are experimenting with single-party and non-parliamentary forms of government as a means of achieving political and monetary stability.

It may now be said that the classical military dictatorship, "the man on horseback", that was once a characteristic of Latin American politics has virtually disappeared. The problem today is no longer a simple conflict between the principles of parliamentarian and authoritarian rule; nor is the coup d'état of today a heroic deed in defence of democracy —though it has sometimes restored law and order. The more cogent political criteria today are efficiency in administration, in fiscal and monetary management and in the maintenance of stable institutions, including the currency. A democratically elected president, working perhaps with a small or unreliable majority in congress, or with none, is in a very vulnerable position; he and his cabinet ministers may be more imaginative or less restrained than are the members of congress by tradition or by sectional—or simply personal—interests; the resistance of the legislature to executive reform may indeed make efficient government difficult or impossible.

The impatience of imaginative presidents with obstructive congresses and self-important party politicians is understandable; moreover, whatever traditional views about the stabilising effect of the legislative branch may be held in London or Washington, presidential impatience and congressional instability are integral parts of the Latin American political scene and must be taken into account. These obstacles to efficiency suggest that the future of the Latin American political structures may tend to be authoritarian. This would be in keeping with Mediterranean tradition and would enable progressive and professional executives to carry out necessary reforms that in Latin America are impracticable under democratic systems.

It can hardly be coincidence that the political structures that seem most likely to survive and prevail to the end of the century are exemplified in the three countries of greatest economic achievement—Mexico, Brazil and Argentina. Mexico has developed the concept of the political party as a powerful regulator; in a virtually single-party system, the Partido Revolucionario Institucional exercises a strong influence on government policies by its choice of the man who is certain to be elected president, and by the advisory activities of its council. The Brazilian two-party system never pretended to be democractic in the European sense; the suspension by decree suggests that the constitutional experiment begun in 1964 has not yet found its definitive form. A genuine and workable pattern of efficient government will undoubtedly emerge, but it is unlikely to be a "traditional" parliamentary system. Argentina has taken the wholly uncompromising line of making no pretence at any party system or popular representation. The Argentine pattern appears to be evolving into a strong military-civilian partnership of undoubted technical ability; its unrepresentational character is accepted in the light of its outstanding practical success.

It can be foreseen therefore that by 1999 the aims of economic growth and social advancement will have been given precedence in Latin America over all other considerations, and that the party politics of earlier decades may be almost forgotten. It should be remembered, however, that the Latin Americans differ from the Anglo-Saxon peoples in their Roman preference for centralism in politics and society; they are not given to federalism or the delegation of power but prefer absolute sovereignty in no matter how small a territory. A political federation of Latin American states on the North American model is most unlikely to occur within the foreseeable future, but this is not to say that the countries will remain economically fragmented; there will almost certainly be two or three successful trading blocks which may be linked in an effective free trade area or even a common market almost wholly independent of the U.S.A.

It follows from these suppositions that the prospect in Latin America is not one of increasing liberality of government; indeed, in a world disturbed by so many profound changes, the Latin Americans will need more, rather than less, self-discipline. It is, however, foreseeable that their governments will become increasingly efficient, and therefore credible, at a time when the reverse has been occurring in Western Europe. It is worth recalling that Brazil, Mexico, and the other Latin American countries are among the few major areas of the world where it matters not at all what colour a man's skin is; by 1999, or sooner, the region has every prospect of becoming a haven of peaceful development and economic strength in a world of bitter racial hatreds and inhuman discriminations.

The important element that will determine the pace at which Latin America's development catches up with and overtakes that of Europe and even the U.S.A., lies in the greater awareness of Latin American political leaders and policy makers of the immense social importance of opportunity. Inadequancy of opportunity has been one of Latin America's characteristics for generations and accounts for many of today's social and political problems. It now seems likely that the coming years may see the evolution of economic policies in Latin America specifically designed to multiply opportunities for the less privileged. The problem is one that is also becoming increasingly evident in Europe and the U.S.A. as younger people challenge the attitudes of their elders and seek greater openings than have previously been available to them; but it is doubtful whether any of the developed countries still retains sufficient economic elasticity to emulate Latin American policies in this regard.

We should be chary of accepting without question the idea that North European and Anglo-Saxon civilisation is superior to the Latin; it has not always been so, and there must be grave doubts about a society that breeds within itself racial prejudice, extreme materialism and permissiveness leading to comprehensive amorality. It is foreseeable that between now and 1999 the authoritarian and probably puritanical reaction, perhaps of draconic severity, will alternate with liberal and reformist forces; society as we have known it in Northern Europe and North America is in danger of being convulsed by this conflict. At the same time, the Latin Americans are becoming known as a group of determined, resourceful and creative nations facing an impressive economic and social advancement; they are the southern half of the New World and their ability to make it a new world in every sense is beyond question.

TRANSFORMATION OF THE MONETARY SCENE

By the spring of 1961 an uneasy calm had been restored in the international currency markets, but the upheavals of the previous year had transformed the prospect: the world's payments system never again settled down to real calm for long, and the search for new solutions was intensified. The upheavals of the period had been too unsettling to be forgotten: the massive flow of hot money into D-marks leading to revaluation of mark and guilder; the panic flight from dollars into gold which caused a steep rise in the gold price on the free London market; and yet another flight from sterling.

Bolton's comments on the various aspects of the crisis characteristically pointed away from technical problems to underlying causes. One cause, it seemed to him, was the immobilisation of capital in Europe, which had not yet found ways of mobilising its new-found financial strength for the benefit of the world at large. He saw the main obstacle in the persistence of Exchange Controls, and he said so very plainly in January 1961 when he spoke at the annual banquet of the Overseas Bankers' Club, a regular climax of the City's social year at which bankers and officials from many countries attend. Bolton was taking the place of the absent Governor of the Bank of England, and he spoke on Exchange Control as a man known to have unique experience of the subject. He roundly condemned these payments restrictions as harmful and unnecessary, and urged that the financial organisations of Europe should be allowed to mobilise their combined resources.

I propose to be controversial, even rebellious, in the presence of this impressive gathering of European political, official and banking talent. What I want to say is basically connected with the current argument between the Six and the Seven, but I am in no way attempting to speak as an expert on this particular subject—still less do I wish to comment on Britain's relationship to either one of these groups.

This controversy has gone on for a long time, and will probably continue, while the field is left to those dedicated representatives of electorates who are accustomed to think only in terms of national sovereignty. In the meantime, the general situation in Western Europe has changed radically. The long period of post-war reconstruction is now over, but we in Western Europe find it difficult to adjust ourselves to that fact. After many years of crisis, it is difficult to recognise prosperity for what it is. It is still harder to accept and act on Europe's changed position in relation to the rest of the Western World. The last few years have brought immense increases in wealth, industrial strength and monetary capacity. At the same time, especially during the last two years, people have become increasingly aware of Europe's obligations towards the under-developed countries and of her capacity to help them.

Much has been said and written about the world-wide hunger for capital, and it is true that complex industrial civilisations generate an almost limitless demand for further capital. However, it is now becoming apparent that Europe's investment potential is not being used to the full; in my opinion, the reason for this is neither the divisions between the various national sovereignties, although these play their unfortunate part, nor the prospect of a trade war between the Six and the Seven. The real cause, I believe, is the persistence of exchange controls, the restriction over the movements of people and the consequent granulation of Europe's capital and human resources into isolated jealous particles.

European exchange controls stem from the great depression and the second world war. They fulfilled an essential function during the immediate post-war difficulties. That period is over, and yet many controls are still maintained largely for the purpose of restricting investment abroad in order to retain as much as possible for domestic purposes.

I suggest that this is inconsistent with the situation today, for three reasons:- firstly, it ignores the increase in Europe's wealth and resources in relation to the rest of the free world. Secondly, it fails to take into account Europe's responsibilities towards the underdeveloped countries; it is clear that the capital resources of the U.S.A. are not limitless and that Europe can no longer leave entirely to them the provision of the investment and development capital which the backward countries desperately need. The so-called "population explosion" in those countries is bound to exacerbate the chronic shortage of savings for investment, unless foreign capital is forthcoming to create a fertile soil for future growth. I believe that Europe would be more aware of its capacity to respond to this need if collaboration between the financial centres were made possible. And thirdly, the divisions created by European exchange controls are out of keeping with the underlying pretensions of both the Six and the Seven—both of which aim, ultimately, at a greater degree of economic integration and a diminution of national sovereignty.

I am convinced that the financial organisations of Europe—public, quasi-public and private—should be allowed, and indeed encouraged, to get together to mobilise their combined financial resources and human talents.

Accordingly, I urge that Britain should take the lead in encouraging the financial organisations of Europe to act in unison. Europe could then make a major contribution to development programmes in all parts of the world, with obvious benefits both to the underdeveloped countries themselves and to world trade in general. At the same time, Europe could expand its own basic industries, keep them up to concert pitch and thus contribute towards the fulfilment of national policies of full employment. Between us we might also go some way towards solving the problem of medium term credit for export of capital goods.

I therefore ask our guest speaker, the Chancellor of the Exchequer, to take very seriously a plea to abandon British Exchange Controls and much of the restriction over the free movement of people, and to encourage other European Governments to do likewise.

The next salvo was fired at a meeting of the Lombard Association, an important City dining club composed mainly of bankers and bank officials operating in the international money market. Again he deplored the slow progress of Europe in organising effective capital markets, and declared that the Western World faced greater danger in the exchange situation than in the military field. He criticised "stupid anachronisms, such as exchange controls which demonstrably do not control exchanges" and rejected "academic" proposals for floating exchange rates—a subject in which he had gained practical experience in the early thirties. A system of constantly moving exchange rates, he said, "means a life of constant agitation throughout the international banking system, and a tendency . . . for finance and trade to be dropped in favour of gambling in the exchanges and in commodity markets." This verdict is particularly interesting in view of Bolton's support for a temporary floating exchange rate in the emergency situation of 1952, which was described on pages 25-26.

Europe is an example of the stimulus resulting from disaster. If Western Europe could be persuaded to integrate and co-ordinate its currencies, its banking systems and capital markets, it could rival if not overtake the capacity of the U.S.A., and far exceed the efforts of Russia which, from the point of view of mobilisable capital, is a poor country.

There is, at last, a growing recognition in Europe that the countries that have made rapid economic progress, and have acquired considerable reserves—assisted by U.S. finance—should assume a greater share of responsibility for the growth of the emergent countries, and should return their surplus funds into international circulation in the form of economic aid.

But this is much easier said than done, and the machinery available in European capital markets either does not work, as in London, or is non-existent, as in Germany. In London, the Foreign Bond Market has collapsed under the impact of the breakdown of the market in British Government Stocks, and the situation has been made worse by the general suspicion of investment in fixed interest bearing securities. The lack of creditworthiness of many borrowing countries has been a contributory factor, but is not the whole cause.

Germany, on the other hand, has not had a bond market since 1918, and German capital markets are today entirely under the control of the deposit banks, who have their own technical reasons for avoiding substantial investment in long term bonds.

Apart from Government sponsored schemes, again dependent upon each government's domestic credit or upon taxable capacity, there is no easy method of channelling European savings into the raw material producing countries where they are most needed.

I would now like to turn to the exchange situation, where more danger faces the Western World than in the military field. The gold crisis of October 1960 and the exchange crises of February 1961 have emphasised the need for measures to promote exchange stability. The hot money and investment movements which occur at times of exchange tension serve to aggravate existing problems. These conditions direct capital into speculative employment which otherwise would have been committed to more useful commercial channels. The prospect of periodic eruptions in international exchanges encourages capital to take advantage of the speculative conditions that are offered from time to time, and this can only be to the detriment of banking credit for commerce, and to longer term foreign investment. The effect of chronic anxiety will ultimately be reflected in contracting world trade.

There has recently been ample scope for the speculative employment of capital—building up with the flow of hot money into Germany during 1960, and with the pressure on the dollar brought into the open last October. The German and Dutch revaluation in February brought anything but equilibrium to the exchange markets and, in fact, set off speculation based upon the possibility of more revaluation. One immediate result was a massive flow of hot money to Switzerland, followed by a speculative attack on sterling. We are now faced with a situation where the maintenance of equilibrium in international exchanges is vital if the capital wealth of the Western World is to be mobilised for the industrial development of the underdeveloped countries. There now appears to be a superficial lessening of the tensions between the currencies of the West. The drain on the U.S. gold reserves has been halted, the raid on sterling is over, and interest rates in the open market are becoming more normal. Suggestions are made, from time to time, that the general structure of exchange rates in Europe no longer reflects the relative values of the currencies concerned, and that stability would be achieved by a general realignment.

I believe the time has come when European bankers should insist that they can combine to the advantage of Europe as a whole, and provide short and medium term credit for all purposes connected with domestic and foreign trade. Cash and credit should be put to work for trade and commerce, and not for purely financial manipulation. We should constantly agitate against stupid anachronisms, such as exchange controls which demonstrably do not control exchanges, and which provide a happy hunting ground for privilege.

I would also ask you to pay attention to the structure of the international exchanges. It is quite impossible, in modern circumstances, to say whether one paper currency should at any time be worth more or less than any other paper currency, in terms of official rates of exchange. There is a clamour from time to time that one currency or another should be adjusted. It should either be revalued in terms of all the others, or devalued in terms of all the others; and, when the underlying anxieties come to the surface, we experience something in the nature of an exchange crisis. We have had at least three in the last six months. I believe that, if the capitalist system is to succeed in standing up to the pressure of collectivism under central control, it must avoid exchange disturbances of recent magnitudes.

There are a large number of academic protagonists of moving exchange rates as a method of dealing with these recurrent crises. A number of us here have had experience of constantly moving exchange rates, and I would say, on my own behalf, that this is not a system that can prevail. It means a life of constant agitation throughout the international banking system, and a tendency, which becomes more pronounced as time goes on, for finance and trade to be dropped in favour of gambling in the exchanges and in commodity markets.

A matter of great importance was introduced quietly at a recent weekend meeting of the Bank for International Settlements in Basle. The European central banks have agreed to help to maintain stability and by joint action to frustrate speculation and temporary market movements. I believe that the fact that the European central banks have been thrown into each other's arms, as a result of the exchange panic that followed the modest revaluation of the Deutsche mark and the Dutch guilder, has great importance for the future. If the European central banks agree to support each other's currencies, then the current pattern of exchanges will be maintained, and speculation will prove to be unprofitable. Surplus money will tend to circulate in Europe for rational reasons, and not under the dual impulses of fear and greed.

The embryonic market which is erroneously called Euro-dollars will develop in these circumstances into a European money market, which will prove to be of great benefit to Western Europe as a whole. The fact that European monetary authorities, under the pressure of events, have been impelled to come together, means that breathing space will be bought, and what have appeared to be insoluble problems—such as the growth of Western European monetary reserves at the expense of the American monetary reserves—will be dealt with quietly and intelligently. I feel that it behoves all international bankers to do everything they possibly can to help restore order in the exchanges. It is high time that the Western World understood that a unified military strategy cannot succeed without agreement on a common monetary policy.

> About the same time in 1962 (in his annual Review of events in the previous year) he sounded a theme which remained constant in his mind ever since: that the capitalist world must restore public confidence in the paper currency system if it is to preserve the political and social freedoms of democracy. He saw no alternative to this harsh task either in exchange rate adjustments or in the restoration of some variant of the gold standard. Monetary stability had to be secured, if necessary, by changes in foreign and military policy. But this dilemma of the United States and Britain was unfortunately not understood in continental Europe, which dwelt smugly in "self-centred indifference".

The trading and financial world is experiencing many discomforts derived from anxieties over international politics, from doubts regarding the world's major currencies and their related problems, and from confused thinking about overseas trade. It is practically impossible to isolate and define all the various forces at work; but certain situations are now emerging more clearly. Among these is the end of the apparently automatic expansion of world trade that began in 1945; the industrial nations' foreign trade has become increasingly dependent on the expansion of capital investment in existing and new industries, and on replacement demand rather than on new direct consumption; it has also been affected by a slowing of the rise in the average living standards of the major trading countries.

Attention is belatedly being given to the effects on world trade of the continuous fall in commodity prices over the last decade; this has brought about exchange and payments disturbances and internal financial and monetary problems in virtually every country that is dependent on the export of primary products. These difficulties have affected the whole of South and Central America and Africa, with the exception of the Republic of South Africa, which enjoys a steady income from the export of gold and diamonds. and in one way or another their consequences have been felt throughout the Commonwealth.

Besides these trading problems, and partly as a consequence of them, there is now a deeply-rooted lack of confidence in the structure of foreign exchanges. Not only trading difficulties, but also the continuing heavy military and foreign aid expenditure by the U.S.A. and, to an equivalent but lesser extent, by the United Kingdom is affecting the stability of both the dollar and sterling. These currencies are under remorseless pressure, as is revealed from time to time by events in the exchange markets. It is an inherent distrust of these and other paper currencies that is the underlying factor in the gold price controversy; yet it should be obvious that the philosophy of the freedom of the individual cannot be translated into such freedom as we actually enjoy today unless there is confidence in paper currency systems.

An alternative to the present mechanism is not to be found in a return to a variant of the gold standard, for the simple reason that there is not enough gold to go round. Nor can any immediate solution be found in the creation of a universal money issued through an international authority; this may prove to be the ultimate solution but it is too remote, in the context of current international frictions, to be a practicable possibility in the foreseeable future. The only likely alternative to our present system would be a relapse into dictatorship, of the extreme Left or Right, accompanied by State control of all economic activities and complete loss of the freedom of the individual.

The countries of the Western World are attempting, individually and haphazardly, to deal with these problems but in most cases their approach is coloured by self-regarding domestic policies and inherited concepts of national prestige. The U.S.A. is a notable exception; despite a large budget deficit and an increasingly adverse payments position reflected in heavy outflows of gold, the U.S. Government continues to bear the larger part of the Western World's defence burden and to lead in the provision of aid to developing countries. How long this situation will continue must depend on the patience of the United States taxpayer and on the wisdom of the Europeans, who have been among those who have benefited most from United States aid and military expenditure.

Unfortunately financial opinion in continental Europe is highly critical of both British and United States monetary policies, and is at the same time insistent on the political necessity of Britain and especially the U.S.A. maintaining, at their own expense, substantial military establishments abroad, particularly in Europe. An unpleasant dilemma is arising. The strain imposed on both the dollar and sterling by the political and defence commitments of the U.S.A. and Britain is painfully evident when one looks at the international payments positions of these two countries. To protect their currencies, both Washington and Whitehall may be faced with the need to make decisions on the relative importance of their foreign and military policies and monetary stability.

The Europeans seem to have retained a certain self-centred indifference to the state of the two major international currencies. The recent agreement reached in Vienna to strengthen the resources of the International Monetary Fund has not been enthusiastically received in some European financial circles, and it probably represents the limit of the concessions that the European countries are willing to make. The modest reforms that were accepted in Vienna may enable the I.M.F. to correct short term distortions in the exchange situation, but they fall short of ensuring that the Fund could with equanimity face a major convulsion; and they do not create any additional liquidity for the expansion of world trade.

The problem of world liquidity is rendered the more intractable by recurrent weakness in the two principal international currencies. The immediate danger facing the dollar lies in the day-to-day responsibility of the Secretary of the Treasury to supply gold to foreign monetary authorities at U.S. $35 an ounce, and in his indirect responsibility to keep the price of gold in free markets as close as possible to the official price. The argument as to whether $35 an ounce is the right price for gold is irrelevant in a situation where the U.S.A. has not sufficient gold to meet current and potential demands, and where the world has shown a preference for gold, even though it is expensive to hold and store.

In these circumstances, international credits and I.M.F. stand-by facilities are of only modest value; there are no really valid alternatives, as international currencies, to dollars and sterling cleared through the financial centres of New York and London. However strong the

Deutsche Mark, French franc, Italian lira, or Swiss franc may appear to be, none of the countries in question has the machinery or the will to take on the burden of being one of the world's bankers. It is also clear that, in certain of these European countries, the basic social and political stability that is essential if international credit is to be maintained over long periods is at present lacking and is unlikely to be achieved in the near future.

The outstanding problem today is not whether the price of gold should be raised, nor whether sterling or the dollar should be devalued, nor whether the Deutsche Mark or the Italian lira should be revalued, nor whether exchange rates should float or have wider official quotations. It is to be found in the fact that the tremors, large and small, that pass across the exchanges are no longer a reflection only of the weaknesses or follies of any particular government; they are the consequences of many years' abuse of the paper money system. While the air is filled with the sounds of academic controversy about ways out of every difficult situation, that disregarded victim, the common man, is increasingly showing a healthy distrust of economic expedients accompanied by showers of paper money of ever-declining value.

The disasters—economic, monetary, social and political—which Bolton predicted in the early sixties did not, in fact, occur at that time. They were averted, or perhaps only postponed, by two events which neither he nor any one else had allowed for. One was the utterly unexpected halt in American inflation, which resulted in virtual stability of U.S. prices between 1960 and 1964 and some cautious revival of confidence in the dollar abroad; the second new factor was the rapid development of the international (Euro-dollar) money and capital market as a new source of liquidity for international trade, finance and capital investment.

It was the second of these events in which Bolton had been actively involved since the tentative beginnings in 1957, and in July 1962 he made his first public assessment of the potential importance of the Euro-dollar mechanism. Incidentally, he argued against persistent support by central banks of the forward exchange market "as an alternative to some simple, though painful, reforms of the monetary and budgetary policies of their governments". He was not to know until later that the British government took the opposite decision in the November 1964 sterling crisis, with consequences which bore out Bolton's warnings.

The consequences of decisions in the political sphere have been felt progressively in the economic field and they have subsequently had their effects on the solidity of the reserve currencies. Non-American and non-British holders now enjoy a large and growing supply of dollars, and sterling holdings still remain substantial. Stronger reserve situations have been built up in countries such as Germany, the Benelux group, Italy and France, which have been less affected than Britain and the United States by both the domestic and the international pressures that have dictated U.S. and British policies. In addition, the local cash surpluses on the Continent tended to become more difficult to place as they increased in volume and found no outlet in local markets. Despite the assumed flexibility of the New York and London money markets, strains have become manifest as a result of this growing volume of foreign exchange, and a looser organisation has grown up and now operates at rates of interest that are established by a completely free market and are not subject to central bank supervision or control. In many dollar-surplus countries dollars tend to remain in private hands and, in fact, many European central banks have at times done everything possible to avoid buying surplus dollars from their domestic banks.

These developments have greatly increased the activity of foreign exchange markets and have brought about a growth of the forward exchange market largely as a result of surplus funds endeavouring to move from one centre to another with the minimum of exchange risk. In the course of the development of this embryonic international money market, interest rates for sterling and dollar deposits have tended to fluctuate with the volume of supply and demand, the level of forward exchange rates, and the rates of interest current outside the official New York or London markets. While the official money market rates play a determining part in setting the general level of interest rates in the international money market, it is significant that the movement of money does not flow through old-established channels. Because of the official regulations in the U.S.A. and accepted practices among the clearing banks in London, the various participants in these two money markets are precluded from dealing in the international money market. Their place has been filled by a mixture of overseas banks and the offices of foreign banks, and to some extent, the larger industrial organisations that have a high degree of liquidity.

A parallel development is the growing practice of large industrial corporations in the U.S.A. and continental Europe to participate in the exchange of surplus cash resources between themselves without the intervention of domestic banks.

When these activities first developed, it was thought that the limits that practically every bank establishes on every other bank for forward exchange contracts would ultimately restrict the market. It was also felt that making deposits for periods varying from one day up to one year between banks would have some natural limitation and the market would reach saturation in a relatively short time. However, this has not occurred for a variety of reasons, notably because the composition of the market now includes institutions whose credit rating in some cases could not be measured by either traditional or practical standards. For example, the leading British local government authorities, as a result of credit squeezes and high money rates, were left in a position where recourse to the London capital market represented a remote hope and not a reality. To meet their growing liabilities, the various local government Treasurers, who had been in the habit of taking short-term money in the form of local mortgages, were in a position, if they paid high enough rates, to take deposits from seven days up to one year or more; and as deposits were paid off others were offered to them. There is no doubt whatever that some of the short-term liabilities of the local authorities have a foreign exchange origin.

The hire purchase companies, when they became associated with or controlled by the clearing banks, also found that their credit standing was such that they could compete for this kind of money, and very large sums have been deposited with them through the operations of the international money market. The market was also broadened by the Canadian chartered banks and the London and European offices of the leading United States banks, which were anxious to accept deposits, partly through a desire to have a position in this international market and partly so as to keep up the deposit figures of each bank as a whole.

We have now reached a situation where hundreds of the leading banks of the world are engaged in depositing money with each other, without security, at rates of interest that are affected but not determined by the margins of the official money rates prevalent in the New York and London markets. This has been accomplished within the last ten years entirely as a result of international needs, the enterprise of the banks, the confidence they have in each other and the fact that the main money markets have become too much subject to domestic requirements and political direction. There seems little doubt that, through the passage of time, and in the absence of any change in the procedures of the official money markets, this international market will affect domestic money rates. It is scarcely accurate to describe these activities as hot money movements, as the money has been created by monetary authorities and is part of the resources of the financial system; it does not represent speculation, and if there appears to be too much money on current account in international circulation government policies over the post-war period are mainly responsible.

It is clear that, unless all governments were to agree to isolate their monetary systems from each other, this kind of activity has come to stay. It is probable that the supremacy of the official New York and London money markets has now passed and is unlikely to return, unless these two markets were to absorb the newly created international money market. This would not be an easy thing to do, nor would it necessarily be the right thing to do. It is quite possible that, in the same way that Britain has created an external and an internal sterling, it is advisable to have an international as well as an internal money market. An important matter, from Britain's point of view, is whether London remains the centre, or a leading centre, in these activities. They not only provide profits with the minimum expenditure of resources and energy, but they also provide Britain with a financial capacity that the sterling system cannot itself generate. The additional capacity incidentally helps to finance British and sterling area exports.

The efficient operation of this free market in money depends upon the existence of a comprehensive market in forward exchange. There has been a tendency over recent years for financial journalists and economic commentators to suggest that there is a technical way out of monetary and exchange difficulties through the use by central banks of forward exchange markets. There is no doubt that gerrymandering the forward exchanges is a technical device that can be used to some advantage by central banks from time to time; but if the central banks are to lend their name permanently to forward exchange operations in any of the leading currencies, then they will vastly increase the scope of these markets and incidentally make the path of the speculator, who does occasionally emerge, much easier than need be. It has been mentioned earlier that most banks impose some limits on their activities in foreign currency deposits and forward exchange operations and in the volume of transactions with each individual bank. A central bank, by definition, has no such limitation in its own market; transactions between central banks probably have limitations but if all the central banks were to be engaged in this kind of operation, the velocity of foreign exchange turnover could substantially increase and the volume of transactions could be magnified out of all proportion to business and financial needs.

Danger could come, however, from a different direction, namely in the event of alarm growing about the financial position of any one country. If the outstanding volume of transactions in both exchange and foreign deposits had greatly increased internationally as the result of central bank operations, the point could be reached at which the markets might virtually come to a standstill, accompanied by disconcerting movements in forward exchange margins and interest rates. It is to be hoped, therefore, that whatever the central banks may do in this field, they will not regard it as an alternative to some simple, though painful, reforms of the monetary and budgetary policies of their own governments.

The confidence that exists among members of the international banking system is as strong as each individual link in a chain. The central banking community, while carrying out its responsibilities for the soundness and value of national currencies, should not overlook the fact that the currency in a modern state does not exist apart from the domestic and foreign banking system, and that no banking system in the western world can be treated in isolation from any other.

Monetary arguments took a new turn in 1962, when the British Chancellor, Reginald Maudling, submitted to the annual meeting of the I.M.F. in Washington the first of a series of schemes designed to "increase international liquidity" by creating a new type of paper reserve asset for use in payments between central banks. His plan for a "mutual currency account" was coldly rejected by the U.S. administration, but it gave a start to the prolonged discussions which by 1969 produced agreement on the "Special Drawing Rights". In February 1962 the British authorities had similarly frowned on an American scheme (backed by the German, Swiss and

Italian central banks) for short-term "swap" facilities to be arranged between the Federal Reserve Bank of New York and European central banks as a means of mutual support against speculative pressures. This modest scheme, devised as a stop-gap by a group of central bank exchange dealers, turned out to be the main shield against currency collapse in the succeeding seven years. By May 1963 the Treasury and Bank of England had belatedly recognised its potential use and agreed to a mutual standby facility with the "Fed" of up to $500 million. That, of course, was only the beginning.

The U.S. payments deficit widened again in 1963, and in July various measures to restore balance were announced, including an interest equalisation tax on foreign loan and stock issues in the American capital market. This was intended to reduce the pressure of borrowers on the New York market, which had increased enormously in the previous year. In that objective it was successful. But in barring the New York market to the great majority of potential foreign borrowers, the restrictions set in motion another development: they gave the City of London, and later the European banking system, a chance of organising a new international capital market for governments, local authorities and international companies now excluded from the New York market.

In an article written for the London "Times" (published September 30, 1963) Bolton deplores the additional American retrictions (ordinary U.S. bank lending overseas had been restricted earlier) and appeals to the British government to lose no time to restore the London capital market.

The American administration has recently instituted a variety of measures to protect the United States gold reserve from further erosion and to support the exchange rate of the dollar. Restrictive action is inevitable while American foreign policy necessitates continued and substantial expenditure abroad, the net result of which is to add to the volume of dollar balances in foreign hands and, in the long run, to diminish the gold reserve.

The United States can take very few steps in the monetary field without influencing the western world as a whole, and one of the more recent proposals is likely, if approved by Congress, to damage the efficiency of the international monetary system and the working of international capital markets. The tax proposals now before Congress, designed to discourage American portfolio investment in foreign securities and issues on the New York market, cannot fail to have long term effects, some of which can be foreseen.

The world is in danger of moving into a system of monetary areas inside which capital flows fairly freely, but between which capital investment may tend to be made difficult by regulation or other pressures. The sterling area is the oldest and best known of the restrictive monetary areas, but it is being followed by the communist area known as COMECON. The six countries included in the E.E.C. are in course of developing a closed system; and now a dollar area composed substantially of North and South America and some part of Africa, inside which long term capital investment in dollar terms will apparently be unregulated by the American authorities, has begun to appear. How far these developments represent a granulation of the world into opposing groups in the economic field, in addition to the political antagonism between the western world and the communist group of countries, is difficult to forecast with any accuracy; but in view of the exchange tensions that exist and major differences of opinion on monetary policy, there seems to be little doubt that, as the monetary areas become more efficiently organised, friction will develop between them.

Ever since 1939, the world has in large measure been deprived of many of the older capital markets and, for a lengthy period in many centres, even short term banking transactions were actively discouraged or entirely prevented by the operation of exchange and other controls.

During the post-war period, exchange controls have been gradually relaxed in terms of the finance of foreign trade and tourism. Even portfolio investment is now becoming respectable. Between 1939 and 1963, however, there were only two international capital markets available to all comers, namely Zurich and New York, the latter being immeasurably the larger and better organised market. Additions to the scope of these two centres have been made by international organisations such as the World Bank, I.F.C., etc. One of the effects of the projected American legislation will be largely to eliminate New York as a source of long term capital, except on a semi-charitable basis, as the majority of the countries allowed unlimited access to the New York market have an indifferent credit status.

The international organisations, in view of their constitutions and procedures, cannot take the place of New York, and in fact, there has been a noticeable slowing down of their investment in new projects over the past few years.

The mere fact that certain countries enjoy a favourable balance of payments and have rising exchange reserves does not mean that they can automatically take the place of New York. Free capital markets develop over generations, and are dependent upon a highly sophisticated and complex organisation which is expensive to maintain and which is always short of trained and experienced personnel. The international capital market depends upon a community which essentially takes the long view of the inherent risks of foreign investment, and which accepts international responsibilities, as well as the more popular but narrower domestic responsibilities.

While, therefore, the measures taken against foreign investment and foreign issues by the American administration may be justified by the condition of the dollar, from a long term point of view they could turn out to be an unmitigated disaster for the western world unless some alternative is developed. A partial alternative in terms of organisation, attitudes and experience, is the restoration of the London Market, which has retained its international characteristics and efficiency of operation during the long period of stresses and strains of an economic and monetary nature.

Since the end of the war, every British Government has, from the point of view of economic policy, been forced to look inwards and not outwards. This self-regarding policy has been mitigated, to some extent, by the existence of the sterling area, where there has been free movement of both medium and long term capital. However, even the apparent freedom of the sterling area has been qualified by governmental pressure on the independent members of the Commonwealth to raise their capital resources abroad, meaning in this context the United States. This has been followed since 1961 by British corporations being encouraged to raise foreign loans to meet their development needs. These tactics have not been followed by the British Government which makes substantial grants and loans out of sterling resources to previously dependent territories, acting on political and not economic grounds. There is little evidence that these political grants and loans have earned any political benefits, but this is a matter for the government of the day to decide.

However, if loans and aid given to newly independent territories by both the British and American Governments are to have any success in helping to maintain the democratic system with its ideals of the freedom of movement of both individuals and money, then it is essential that some regard should be paid to the financial system which underpins the whole of the western world. Otherwise, there will eventually be very little difference between COMECON, the communist monetary area, whose foreign loan transactions are entirely political in nature, and the western monetary areas either in being or in the process of development. The British Government should, therefore, actively encourage the redevelopment of the London Market to assist in the maintenance of an international monetary system and to discourage, as far as possible, the development of opposing monetary blocks.

The London Market should also be encouraged to act as a catalyst for the mobilisation of European and other financial resources, through devices such as external sterling, the Euro-dollar and the host of other currencies which circulate in the mis-named Euro-dollar market. The international responsibilities of the leading governments incorporated in the sterling and dollar areas, and London and Washington's mutual external political responsibilities, should be re-examined to see how far their positions would become stronger and less exposed if the barriers between the two monetary areas were to be lowered and London and New York given the task of mobilising the capital resources of the whole for the use of all.

The two major monetary authorities have been working closely together for many years, and there is no basic difference between their respective monetary problems. The two main markets—London and New York—are accustomed to combining forces, and many strong links have been forged between financial groups on both sides of the Atlantic. The two systems are inherently non-competitive. In terms of the enormous load which falls upon them for the purpose of financing world trade, and of providing foreign exchange, money and capital markets, their aims and policies tend to move together in a common direction determined by a common purpose.

The present exchange tensions and anxieties about the price of gold would be largely removed if the authorities concerned were publicly to accept the underlying reality: that the dollar and sterling systems are one and that the two currencies are now indissolubly tied to each other.

BRITAIN'S ROLE IN THE WORLD

George Bolton has always seen the problems of banking and finance as part of a large human stage. Political, strategic, economic and social trends are to him mere aspects of a single challenge, and he moves smoothly from one discipline into the other, in private conversation as much as in a formal speech or a written paper. Moreover, he has the ability to see the world in the round. ("I find it difficult", he said on one occasion, "to consider any part of the world in isolation from the rest.") Most men of action—bankers, businessmen, politicians, or soldiers—except perhaps the specialists in Washington and Moscow devising nuclear targets, work on a tacit assumption that the earth is flat. They look at one portion of the globe at a time. Bolton's experience with the sterling area, the creation of the post-war world payments system, the problems of the dollar, and the Latin American economies has given him a three-dimensional vision to which his mobile mind responds joyfully.

The comments which follow were provoked, first by the British application to join the European Economic Community in August 1961, and in the following year, by the Cuba crisis of October 1962.

His first extensive comment on the E.E.C. (of which this quotation is an abridged version) was printed in the BOLSA "Review" for October 1961. At first glance it makes odd reading. Bolton is today regarded as one of the most outspoken opponents of British entry into the E.E.C.; for some years he has lost no opportunity to condemn the repeated efforts of British governments to seek membership, arguing that a much more natural and promising economic association would be with North and South America, the old white Commonwealth and perhaps Japan.

Yet in this first assessment he discussed the movement towards European unity with sympathy and saw many advantages for Britain in joining. He is certainly not one of those insular Britons whom he himself has described as thinking of continentals as "people who do not speak English, who have curious legal systems, whose governments come and go like the unpredictable winds, and who tend to choose Presidents who become dictators". Bolton started his working life in a French bank; he was in constant touch with continental central banks and monetary authorities during the thirties; and he was personally involved in the reconstruction of the continental currencies after the second world war.

Nor was he put off by any exclusive concentration on the Commonwealth or the sterling system. He had long advocated a common currency for Europe and looked for the pooling of European capital resources through the highly developed mechanism of the City of London. In any case his first reaction to Mr. Harold Macmillan's application for Britain to join the E.E.C. was quite favourable. His doubts were quietly expressed in two paragraphs at the end of a thirteen-page, broadly approving essay, and it was only in the last few lines that he disclosed his preference for a "union between the sterling and dollar systems and the respective political organisations" as "a more intelligent conception with greater mutual advantages". A few years (and two French vetoes) later this seed had grown to a full-scale policy.

Aspirations towards unity have been held in Europe at various times from Charlemagne to Napoleon, and more recently Hitler, but the approach has generally been based on the concept of conquest and domination: enforced unification rather than voluntary association. The economic prostration of Europe after the second world war, when the rivalry between Russia and the U.S.A. was already assuming importance, presented a new set of circumstances that called for new political and economic ideas. It is evident that, during the last fifteen years, British statesmen have been slow to appreciate the consequences of the collapse of national prestige and the attraction towards the larger entity of Western Europe.

The Marshall Aid plan for Europe and the establishment of the Organisation for European Economic Co-operation to administer it began a train of economic co-ordination that soon developed political overtones. The European Economic Community that has grown out of the O.E.E.C. is aiming at unification in more than trading matters. When the Rome Treaty was signed in 1957 its ambitious aims seemed, to official British opinion, quite unrealistic. This scepticism was largely the result of a failure to appreciate the fact that the European movement represented the only way out of a dilemma caused by unrealisable national aspirations.

There are justifications and antecedents for Britain's aloofness. Historically, Britain was for so long a great power as centre of the empire, and later mother of the Commonwealth, that association with continental Europe had never seemed necessary or desirable; the fact that Britain has never been invaded since she became a nation has contributed to the development of a mentality that has little in common with that of the continental Europeans whose experience has been so different, particularly in the two world wars. Post-war political instability has also strengthened the European trend towards political integration and the safer future it appears to offer. These factors have been completely absent in Britain.

The feeling of separateness from Europe was further strengthened by the position of equality with the U.S.A. and the U.S.S.R. that Britain acquired in the peace negotiations. This arose in part from Britain's important role in the conduct of the war and in part from the powerful personality of Churchill. As one of the Big Three, and later as one of the three so-called nuclear powers, Britain maintained a special relationship with the U.S.A.

When Churchill said "we must build a sort of United States of Europe" it is probable that he meant not "we" but "you", the continental nations. Later, the attitude of the Labour government to the European Defence Community and the European Coal and Steel Community showed that insularity was not the prerogative of any political party and was indeed an essential feature of British opinion in general. More recently scepticism has given way to a certain reluctance to accept the political implications of the Rome Treaty and the surrender of national sovereignty inherent in the unification of economic policies in the E.E.C. This attitude was the motive force behind Britain's initiative in creating the European Free Trade Association—"the Seven". It was an attempt to obtain the advantages of freer trade in Europe without the political commitments; it was hoped that some form of association between the E.F.T.A. and the European

Common Market created by the E.E.C. would give Britain access to the whole of western Europe without any loss of her traditional status.

The deeply rooted crisis in Britain's own economy has finally brought her to the point where new policies have become necessary. As an island economy, depending to a large extent on being the centre of the Commonwealth, Britain is ceasing to be viable. The large Commonwealth nations that are developing their manufacturing industries are shrinking markets for Britain's traditional cash exports of consumer goods; competition in simple manufactures from low-cost producers such as Hong Kong, India and Pakistan is increasingly felt in Britain, and the development of Commonwealth exports to other regions is making the agricultural producers less dependent on Britain as a market.

Moreover, as a source of capital for development, Britain is no longer able to meet the Commonwealth's growing needs, and the developing countries have been turning to other sources. Apart from sentimental ties—and even these no longer hold in South Africa—the concepts on which the Commonwealth idea is based are losing their economic importance. This trend may be partly cause and partly effect of the British economic crisis; in any case a fundamental change in Britain's status has occurred and contains the threat of continued economic stagnation, which can only mean decline, unless an equally fundamental change of attitude is accepted. It is at last becoming apparent that the dissolution of the empire involved the permanent loss of jobs, foreign trade and invisible exports.

The Government's decision to apply to the six E.E.C. nations for an opportunity to negotiate Britain's entry into the Community is a step which, although obviously taken with some reluctance and arousing widespread opposition, appears to offer some solution of the problem of survival.

The three most commonly voiced objections to Britain's entering the E.E.C are: the probability that acceptance of the Community's common Customs tariff would not only eliminate Commonwealth preferences but would lead to positive discrimination against Commonwealth products; that tariff commitments under the Rome Treaty might not be compatible with those undertaken under the E.F.T.A.; and that the acceptance of the E.E.C. common agricultural policy would be harmful to British farmers.

These are perfectly valid points. But they are by no means insuperable difficulties: not only can they be overcome, but any sacrifices that they might entail would be more than compensated by the advantages of membership of the Community.

It is obviously impossible to foresee the outcome of future negotiations, but there can be little doubt that, since the E.E.C is in any case a large importer of Commonwealth produce, the final effect on Commonwealth trade will be less profound than has commonly been suggested.

Britain's obligations to the other members of the E.F.T.A. are largely a matter of tariff agreements and therefore subject to negotiation. The probability that Denmark will obtain membership of the E.E.C., as might Norway also, would reduce the importance of E.F.T.A. agreements.

The structure of Britain's argicultural protection policy and the differences between it and the principles in force among the Six are more complex but are not insuperable difficulties. The strong opposition expressed by the National Farmers' Union seems to be dictated more by emotion than by a knowledge of the facts.

The pattern of agricultural protection emerging among the Six is based on policies already in existence in individual countries. It achieves minimum farm prices by tariffs: this tends to make food dearer for the consuming public, but on the other hand there are no taxes for subsidies. Imports of food products by individual members of the Six are affected by quota restrictions and internal taxes as much as by tariffs.

It has been objected that the adoption by Britain of the E.E.C. policy will mean dearer food all round. In fact, only certain items will be affected and the overall rise in the cost of living in Britain would not be great. In theory, there would be a lowering of taxation. The income of farmers as a group would not be affected, although there might be some reduction of marginal farming or amalgamations of uneconomically small holdings. These are processes of adjustment that would in any case be desirable in the interests of agricultural efficiency.

It is not at all clear whether the reiteration of these three points reflects the Government's only preoccupations, or whether it conceals other anxieties that are less suitable for public discussion. Membership of the E.E.C. would imply for Britain—as it does already for the present members—acceptance of political positions that are not all subscribed to enthusiastically by British opinion. For example, the Federal German government's demand for the reunification of Germany is probably less to British taste than a negotiated compromise would be.

A question must also arise on whether Britain's close political association with the E.E.C. would affect Anglo-Russian relations—hitherto, we like to think, a stabilising factor in the fluctuations of the cold war. In contexts such as these, it seems unfortunate that Britain should have waited so long to form a desire to join the Community. If membership had been achieved earlier, before European attitudes hardened, Britain's voice might have had some influence.

There must be yet other reservations in British official thinking that suggest a certain need for caution: for example, the effects of integration on some of Britain's highly protected industries; the effects on the rigid trade union structure of Britain, not only of commercial competition, but also of labour migration.

The objection, not so far very widely discussed, that Britain would be obliged to enter into political and other undefined and possibly unwelcome commitments does not give adequate weight to the fact that Britain is already committed in many respects by her membership of NATO, of the GATT, and of the O.C.E.D., and by participation in the Basle agreement among central banks. On the other hand, if one looks a little beyond the present, it is difficult to see any prospect of social or political stability in several of the countries of the Six. The brittle political structure of Western Germany will be revealed by the inevitable disappearance of Chancellor Adenauer. There is no basic loyalty in the present political parties and the only unifying factors in Western Germany are material gains and fear of Russia. The position of France presents even greater preoccupations because in President de Gaulle is seen the majesty and presence of an eighteenth century figure that cannot have any influence over the future; and his successor, now that so much of the Republican organisation of France has been destroyed by him, might be the French Communist Party, the largest and most powerful Communist group in Western Europe.

In general the Rome Treaty does not lay down lines of policy but only defines objectives and provides institutions: the remarkable speed with which these objectives are being approached reflects the unexpectedly dynamic nature of the institutions responsible for framing policies to attain them. It has become increasingly evident that the economic strength of the Community is now a major factor in world affairs. Britain's continuing aloofness, and the failure of the E.F.T.A. experiment as a means of achieving economic association with the Community without political commitments, now involve certain dangers.

The British economy in its present state of stagnation is no longer able to ensure its own adequate growth nor to be an effective centre of the Commonwealth. The declining dependence of the Commonwealth on Britain, both as a market and as a source of capital, is illustrated by the growth of Commonwealth exports to other regions and the numerous loans that have been obtained from international agencies, from the U.S.A. and from continental Europe.

Finally, industrial costs in Britain have been rising too steeply for British exports to remain competitive: this rise is also at the root of the recurrent inflationary trend. Deflationary measures are seldom more than partially and temporarily effective in a protected economy and appear to be inseparable from stagnation and inadequate capital formation.

The obligation to accept tariff reductions on imports from the Six would provide the painful stimulus that the British economy needs, and in exchange it would achieve compensating advantages in the form of entry for British goods into the E.E.C. market, where purchasing power is expanding. This would not only give efficient and progressive British industries an opportunity to become competitive in a very large market, but it would also significantly reduce the dangers of political reaction to the reduction of tariffs.

The attitude of the trade unions to these prospects is cautious. The T.U.C. has expressed guarded approval of the idea of Britain's entry into the E.E.C., though it notes that the Rome Treaty aims at "a high level of employment" in the Community rather than "full employment". There is naturally some apprehension about the effects of trade competition and the mobility of labour within the Community.

It is almost certain that the influence of this trend would be felt in Britain: further regroupings of companies might be necessary; some trading practices might have to be altered, and some important changes in trade union rules and agreements might be called for. The general effect would inevitably be an imperative need for both management and labour to become more flexible and more efficient than at present. Clearly the adjustments required would vary from one industry to another, and from one company to another, but the enhanced prosperity that would eventually result would be to the advantage of both sides of industry.

These purely common market aspects of the E.E.C. are not the only reasons why Britain's association with the Community is economically desirable. The pooling of financial resources is likely to make Europe a more powerful economic and political bloc than could be possible for the member countries individually.

The E.E.C. has gone a long way in liberating movements of capital, especially funds for direct investments, commerical credits involving residents and dealings in listed securities. In joining the E.E.C. Britain would supposedly have to accept an equal degree of liberalisation.

The question naturally arises whether sterling is at present, or is soon likely to become, strong enough to withstand such liberalisation. Complete freedom would suggest that the exchanges might react more promptly than at present to any trend, whether adverse or favourable; moreover, with Britain closely associated with the E.E.C. the sterling exchange rate with the dollar could be influenced by events in Europe, which might have advantages and disadvantages.

The concept of a common currency in the E.E.C. would remove balance of payments problems among the members, but its successful operation would clearly require a wide degree of integration of monetary policies. It involves the premise that there should be no distortions of purchasing power in different regions—such as may be brought about by inflation in conjunction with fixed exchange rates. A common currency represents absolute rigidity in this context; the possible sources of inflation being various, it is clear that integration or harmonisation would have to be achieved in almost every economic sphere, but it may be supposed that in the eventual conditions of comprehensive integration and complete mobility, regional inflation could occur only in defiance of the wishes and policies of the other members, expressed through the appropriate organisation.

Whatever the exchange and monetary arrangements that might emerge from joining the Six, Britain would have to submit to monetary disciplines that are more acceptable to the European nations than to her own political parties. The marriage of sterling, including the sterling system, with its international responsibility and outlook, with other European currencies operated on gold standard principles is likely to prove an immensely difficult task. This is a major policy problem quite distinct from the matters already mentioned concerning the dismantling of U.K. exchange control.

From the narrower viewpoint of the City, it is probable that with Britain in the E.E.C. there would be an improvement in London's competitive position in relation to the large continental centres. A complex of banking and other financial relations is being built up in the Community, from which London is tending to be excluded. London possesses a more highly developed and skilled banking structure than exists anywhere on the continent, but capital resources are short; the London banks are not able to supply export finance and long term capital on the same scale as banks in the Community. A closer association between the highly organised London banking structure and the capital resources of the E.E.C. would obviously be advantageous on all counts.

Similar considerations may apply to stock market activities. The freeing of capital movements within the E.E.C. and Britain's membership of it could be expected to attract European funds to London's well organised Stock Exchange in response to a large market and high industrial yields. Other activities in the City might also benefit appreciably from integration, which would give scope for their organisation and skill to be developed to the full.

It is still in doubt whether the E.E.C. will become a federation, a confederation or only an economic union with political overtones. In seeking membership of the Community, Britain enters into a number of known economic and undefined political commitments that will bring many problems and will call for so many adjustments of policy and long established practice that, so far as our Constitution is concerned, it is a leap into the unknown.

In accepting the obligations of membership on the political side, Britain may acquire a voice in shaping the future of Europe, and on the commercial side membership of the common market formed by the E.E.C. will provide, through competition, some of the stimulus that is needed to restore Britain's industrial efficiency; at the same time, the reward for efficiency will be access to a large and growing market.

The short term economic and financial arguments in favour of joining appear at first sight to be nearly overwhelming. On the other hand, there are certain aspects of this form of association that are generally overlooked. Britain, together with practically the whole of Western Europe, is an overcrowded area with a high and on the whole rising standard of living, maintained through industrial development. The area as a whole is deficient in raw materials, food and energy resources and, with the decline in imperial power, is tending to lose control of existing raw material production. While becoming a part of the West European trading and financial nexus has short-term attractions, in the long run Britain may find herself in a worse position through a growing dependence of Western Europe as a whole on sources of energy, food and raw materials entirely under non-European control. The area will probably always be industrially efficient, and have a high level of savings, but we shall be putting our faith in the permanent value of our surplus savings (which can only be invested in gold, foreign exchange or extra-European investment) in preference to free access to raw material resources. It is generally forgotten that, through the process of transition from an Empire to a Commonwealth, Britain has been able to maintain banking, trade and investment arrangements with the independent members of the Commonwealth with a minimum of political friction. It is clearly a possibility that entry into Europe will gradually, if not quickly, bring about a major change in the most important and long-standing Commonwealth relationships, namely, with Canada, Australia and New Zealand. This would become all the more certain if the European countries, in their folly, were to attempt to exact humiliating conditions as a price for Britain's entry into the Community.

A more intelligent conception with greater mutual advantages would be, if the political will were there, to form a union between the sterling and dollar systems and the respective political organisations, which would provide a breathing space for our own over-populated island. Expansion possibilities would be limited only by the availability of savings. There is, on the whole, a common heritage of language, laws and customs; the universal use of English as opposed to polyglot continental Europe; the flexible tradition of Anglo-Saxon law as opposed to the rigidities of Roman law; and acceptable political and social systems that have evolved over the ages and stood the test of time, compared with the bleak history of political Europe and the turmoil which seems likely to emerge in the near future.

THE WORLD AFTER CUBA

The Cuba crisis of October 1962 inevitably drew his attention back to the Western hemisphere. He recognised the clash at once as a turning point of world history and thought of its impact, first upon Latin America, then on Europe, and more broadly on the future of great-power relationships. Within a few weeks of the crisis he outlined his ideas on the effect in Latin America to a private meeting in London.

The impact on the American people of the revelation of the extent and speed of the Russian military build-up in Cuba was shattering, and many illusions disappeared overnight. Despite fierce criticism of previous weakness in Washington, the country on the whole was behind the President, and they gladly welcomed support from Britain and Western Europe and South America. The comprehensive support from practically all South American countries can be explained quite simply. With few exceptions, they are all in exchange, social and economic troubles, with the consequent expansion of extreme Left Wing parties actively supported by the Communists. Since the Bay of Pigs fiasco, the apparent lack of courage and direction by Washington and the failure of the Alliance for Progress had brought about a progressive loss of confidence in the survival of the capitalist system.

Possibly an important reason for the calculated risk taken by Moscow in building up a modern armament base in Cuba was to give military support to Communist groups in South America, and effectively to deter the Right Wing groups and convince the waverers of the impending success of Russia. It nearly came off. If the Cuban base had been completed without American resistance, many South American countries would have fallen under Russian influence or actual control, with consequent Russian control over the Pacific and the South Atlantic. I therefore regard President Kennedy's decision to stop Russia at any cost as one of the most important international events since September 1939.

Many important consequences will flow from the success of the American initiative because in spite of the Castro regime continuing in power, its capacity for harm is now severely restricted. The immediate advantages include a revival of confidence in America. This cannot be calculated, but an uplift in morale can have surprising consequences, even in the economic field. Then there is no doubt that the stable elements in Latin America, who were in a state of despair, have been very greatly encouraged; and we can have more confidence in their ability to bring some order out of the present chaos.

There is, of course, much insistence on the need to dispose of Castro by force, and there is obvious danger of Castro, in furious disappointment, creating a situation which would inevitably end in violence. But here we have the curious combination of a joint American/Russian interest in keeping the peace in the Caribbean. If Moscow is to gain anything from this adventure, it is the very long term advantage of securing the survival of the Communist regime in Cuba; hence the negotiated agreement between Kruschev and Kennedy. It is, therefore, in Moscow's interest to force Castro to behave and, if he refuses, to liquidate him. Conversely, despite the ordinary American's chagrin at having to tolerate a Communist government so close to his shores, invasion and liquidation of Castro and his circle of friends would probably wreck America's greatly improved position in Latin America, and revive the fears of Yankee imperialism. It would also provide Washington with the insoluble problem of governing Cuba, as the refugees are hopelessly split, and the capitalist and social organisation of Cuba has been totally destroyed and cannot easily be rebuilt. I believe, therefore, that there is a solid joint American/Russian interest in maintaining the status quo in Cuba.

A fuller appreciation followed in his Review of the Year for 1962 which traced the repercussions of the Cuba confrontation in greater detail. For the present, he believed, the attractions of communism for Latin America had diminished; but the rapidly growing problem of unused resources—human, natural and capital—remained an urgent challenge to the Western World.

Few had thought that the United States government might be prepared to risk nuclear war to defend the U.S.A. From that date, international strategy, politics and economics have undergone a momentous change; most of the forecasts made before October 1962, based on the policies evolved since 1945, must now be reappraised. The struggle between the Western World and Russian-controlled Communist peoples for the domination of the mind of man had brought Moscow to the point of trying to outflank the United States through the fortification of Cuba as an advance base armed with nuclear weapons. If this gamble had succeeded, besides the strategic consequences in North America, many Latin American countries now besieged by financial, economic and social problems would have decided that America had lost the cold war and would have hastened to enter into political and trading arrangements with the Communist countries.

Before October the international political and economic situation had reached dead centre. No strategic movement seemed possible and, in the economic field, the world seemed to be sliding gradually into a state of indecision and depression. This was felt most acutely in the United Kingdom, the U.S.A. and Latin America; even in Western Europe the momentum of the last ten years was dying down. An examination of the Latin American scene illustrates the nature of the tension that exists between the highly integrated industrial communities and the developing countries. The Latin American republics had little choice except between an inefficient capitalist economy, clothed in the rags and tatters of collapsing democracy, and a dictatorship of the left.

The frequent use of the word "development" has tended to obscure the facts. Latin America's needs do not consist only in a shortage of power stations, roads, schools, hospitals or productive equipment; these are more the expressions of economic and social progress than the foundations for it. The key factor in the under-development of Latin America is the largely unused capacity of virtually the whole area, since much the greater part of the human, natural, and capital resources of most of the republics is unemployed.

Latin America's development problems are derived largely from the absence of opportunities that encourage human endeavour. A too rigid social and economic stratification deprives the least privileged people of incentives to produce efficiently; while the large and prosperous urban centres, far from contributing to the improvement of rural life, have grown up at its expense. These two factors are closely connected manifestations of the same basic facts. Although more than half the population of Latin America is engaged in agricultural activity, the various economies are geared to essentially urban civilisations.

One consequence of this division of the population into comparatively prosperous urban conglomerations and depressed rural communities, is inadequacy of food production, with malnutrition in many areas. The situation is aggravated by the fact that the population tends to increase most rapidly in the depressed communities, increasing the pressure on locally inadequate food supplies and accentuating the concealed unemployment. Migratory trends towards the already congested urban centres have created fresh problems. This situation becomes worse each year, and is critical in the light of the estimate that by the end of the twentieth century the population of Latin America will be twice as large as that of North America.

There is one other significant factor in Latin America's development and payments problems; the tendency for the owners of surplus funds to invest them outside their own countries, and for exporters to delay the sale of their exchange earnings. The causes may be various, but the fact is that Latin American liquid capital tends either to be volatile or else to gravitate towards unproductive land speculation. The volume of capital owned by Latin Americans outside their countries is unknown, but various guesses range between U.S.$5,000m. and U.S.$10,000m., and there must be a large amount unproductively invested or hoarded within the various countries themselves. This capital must be included among the region's unused capacities; it may not be enough alone to solve Latin America's basic development problems, but its contribution could be considerable.

The main conclusion that emerges is that the republics, each at its own particular stage, are in a process of ill-balanced evolution. So far, this process has brought little change to the economic and social structure of the republics, with the exception of Mexico and Cuba, and so has passed almost unnoticed, especially in Europe. Without the

Cuban crisis, all developing and underdeveloped countries might soon have been the object of international resolutions followed by the minimum of international action; but in 1963 we are facing a very different world.

The sombre picture of Latin America reflects in certain aspects the condition of other developing countries, labouring under the handicap of shallow-rooted government, low commodity prices, inadequate cash and capital resources, and inefficient administrations burdened with over-ambitious development programmes. There is already evidence, however, that we may expect some improvement following the major change in international politics caused by the Cuban episode and the Sino-Indian border clash. The immediate consequences will be an increase in military expenditure and an inclination by industry to cease its hand-to-mouth buying of raw materials.

There are, however, more important longer-term possibilities which will slowly reveal their influence on the economies of the stronger countries. Both Russia and the U.S.A. had urgent reason for deciding not to fight over Cuba; Russia faced the prospect of a tidal wave of Chinese moving westwards if she were heavily involved in a nuclear conflict; while the United States economy was already under pressure from the growing weight of Washington's armament and strategic programmes.

Washington is using a variety of technical devices to postpone the monetary consequences of the strategic policies of the last ten years; but to postpone the day of reckoning does not solve fundamental weaknesses. The only long-term policy that can effectively banish the spectre of dollar-devaluation is a substantial reduction in military expenditure, both at home and abroad. Now that Washington and Moscow, under current compulsions, have negotiated directly with each other, the two antagonists might possibly consider some mutual reduction in military expenditure which would ease their respective domestic problems. Any movement in this direction will have momentous political consequences, including a decline in the military and political importance of Western Europe. Substantial resources would be released and, if intelligently used, could produce a better balance between the industrial countries and those countries that are struggling with the problems of partially completed development programmes and inadequate domestic and external financial resources.

The outcome of the Cuba crisis suggested the possibility of a new relationship between the United States and the Soviet Union; and Bolton saw quickly that any effort by the two great antagonists to blunt the edge of their conflict and, perhaps, to reduce their armaments would bring about "a decline in the military and political importance of Western Europe".

In a brisk, informal talk to senior naval officers at the Royal Naval College (in January 1963) Bolton told some remarkable stories of little-known monetary war history and then outlined his views on the significance of the sterling system, the need for a common currency for the Western World, and the role to which Britain should aspire in the new world situation.

My outlook on life and my experience are wholly international. I am neither an economist nor a statistician; and, as the Bank of England produces a large proportion of the material used by these dismal pseudo-scientists, over a long life I have come to distrust them. I should also warn you that I regard paper money as an abstraction and not a reality. The pound note costs roughly three-eighths of a penny to design, distribute, collect and destroy, and that is its only real value. The other 19s. 11-5/8pence represents your confidence in your country, its government and institutions.

I have never known or experienced normal financial times, as I began my business life in the chaos which followed the first world war, when the enormous increase in government debt was matched by a corresponding decrease in the value of paper money. This is one of the inevitable consequences of vast military expenditure and of war. England's decision in 1925 to restore the pre-1914 gold standard of sterling was followed by the general strike and a decade of economic depression. The New York Stock Market had boomed steadily from 1914 onwards because of the inflow of foreign money to pay for the war and the consequent stimulus to American industry. The New York Market collapsed in 1929; a series of banking crises resulted, beginning in Austria and Germany, followed by the abandonment of the Gold Standard by England in 1931 and the U.S.A. in 1933. A world depression developed which stimulated the growth of Fascism and Nazism and the rise of Mussolini and Hitler. The culmination of the chronic tensions in financial and other spheres occurred on the 3rd September 1939. When the second world war ended, the paramount position of gold and gold coin as the bulwark and pivot of the world of commerce and banking was destroyed, perhaps for ever, together with the political power of the European empires. Paper money reigned supreme, not because of superior virtue, but because there was no alternative.

I would like to interpolate some monetary war history to show how war and monetary affairs become inextricably mixed. A few of us in the Bank of England were convinced that the rise of the Nazi movement from 1933 onwards made war inevitable, and that the outbreak of war could be dated from 1936 when Hitler took over the Rhineland without any reactions from France and Britain. We then prepared and printed a completely new note issue, as we were aware that the German government were intent on flooding the world with forgeries of pound notes if war broke out. We also, and in defiance of government policy, began a war book and the most important step we took was to organise an exchange and trade control. Among other decisions was a policy of building up gold stocks abroad, but it was not until 1938 that the government took definitive action and allowed us to ship gold abroad by naval vessels. When the King crossed the Atlantic in the "Repulse" escorted by two cruisers, each cruiser carried at today's value some £50 million worth of gold, and it was rumoured that the captain of the one cruiser suffered a nervous breakdown from the triple responsibility of the monarch, keeping station and the gold.

In August/September 1939, we had £750 million afloat in practically any vessel of five hundred tons upwards that was travelling west. None of it was lost. We came to the conclusion in 1940 that we had better get securities out of the country, and eventually shipped some £20,000 million to Canada via the U.S.A. by naval vessels. During the war, we moved some £1,000 million worth of gold over the seven seas and our losses were negligible. In one case, a ship in a convoy off Newfoundland zigged instead of zagged and we lost some £500,000 worth of gold. An explosion in Bombay harbour scattered about £750,000 over the harbour and port area, but we recovered over two-thirds. But the most wonderful episode was the sinking of the "Niagara" with £2 million of gold on board in four hundred and twenty-five feet of water in the Tasman Sea. We recovered all but £100,000 through a remarkable deep sea diving effort.

Gold, because of its stability of value, cost of extraction and the fact that it is universally accepted as a precious commodity, is still very much a tangible asset, and is used between central banks to clear balances. It will continue to be traded internationally, but it has lost its former position as the standard on which the monetary systems of most countries were based. Instead we have paper currencies which are no stronger than the governments and institutions of the countries of issue, and the respect and confidence they inspire generally throughout the world. For this reason, the dollar and sterling emerge as the two leading currencies of the day. They are often referred to as the "reserve currencies", because many countries hold their reserves in them; the bulk of international trade is financed in these currencies and basic commodities are priced in markets conducted in London and New York. Russia, because of Marxist dogma, retains the rouble for internal consumption but her ever-expanding foreign trade is priced and settled in dollars or sterling; and the same is true of most satellite countries. This is one of the many inherent contradictions in the Marxist system, where the denial of the value and transferability of money forces the communists to use the capitalist currencies and trading systems in foreign trade.

The sterling system originated with the industrialisation of Britain during the Napoleonic wars, and progressed steadily as the empire expanded. Raw materials from the empire were returned in the form of manufactured goods, and expanding trade brought with it the establishment of a network of trading companies, banks, merchants and insurance houses through which the wealth then accruing to these islands was channelled. All the accumulated wealth was blown away in two world wars, but the sterling system, with its comprehensive world framework, remains an international financial force of considerable potency. It will continue to play a large part in the world's financial system because of the strength and flexibility of the British banking system, the ability of our international bankers to estimate risks, and world-wide respect for our Constitution.

The political power and industrial potential of the United States was not fully realised until after the first world war, from which it emerged as a chronic creditor nation, and found itself in a position to finance and exploit other parts of the world. In spite of the upheavals to which I referred earlier, the dollar grew, as sterling had done before it, to become an international currency and make New York the place of settlement for an enormous volume of international transactions.

Continental Europe, as you all know, has made a remarkable economic recovery since 1945, and this has been accompanied by a corresponding growth in financial capacity. But the background to their political, social and monetary systems is such that—united or divided—the European countries and currencies are most unlikely to provide the world with a comprehensive international monetary and banking system. Although some west European countries have strong reserve positions, they have no alternative for the next generation or so than to use the dollar and sterling systems. For the strength and flexibility of banking systems is as important, if not more important, than the soundness of the money; and the techniques indispensable to the performance of a world money market are only acquired by inherited aptitudes and many years of experience.

Current monetary policy is organised and conducted by central banks and Treasuries through a variety of mechanisms. The chief of these is the domestic money market which mobilises and offsets the cash resources and claims of the local banking community. The central bank—in our case the Bank of England—uses the market to control the liquidity of the clearing banks; and the issue of Treasury bills and short term government bonds are essential elements in providing security against money market loans. The Bank of England sells them when it wants to take money out of the market and buys them back again when it wishes to ease credit.

Foreign exchange markets, however, are active in all centres, and provide a further and efficient channel through which local cash surpluses in domestic currency can be placed. Currently, London and New York are the two main centres where short term funds can be invested or deposited in practically any volume; although such funds are frequently transferred rapidly to Zurich, Paris or Frankfurt at the slightest suggestion of dollar or sterling difficulties.

The domestic policies of the Bank of England and the Federal Reserve in New York operate largely through the London Bank Rate and New York Discount Rate but, owing to the growing volume of business in recent years in foreign exchange, a looser organisation has grown up in Europe which operates at rates of interest not subject to central bank supervision or control. It is difficult to describe how this so-called

Euro-dollar market works, and how rates are established, as there is a complicated process of spot exchange transactions, forward operations and deposits between banks, and it tends to be highly specialised and technical in operation.

We have now reached a situation where hundreds of leading banks in the world are engaged in depositing money with each other, without security, at rates of interest affected, but not determined, by the official money rates prevalent in London and New York. This has been accomplished in the last ten years, as a result of international needs, the enterprise of the banks and the confidence they have in each other, and also the fact that the main domestic markets have tended to become inflexible besides being subject to political direction and other control.

It is probable that the supremacy of the official London and New York money markets has now passed and is unlikely to return, unless these two markets were to absorb the newly created international money market. This would not be an easy thing to do, nor would it necessarily be the right thing to do. The important matter from Britain's point of view is whether London remains the centre, or trading centre, for these activities. They not only provide profits with the minimum expenditure of resources and energy, but they also provide Britain with the financial capacity that the sterling system alone cannot generate, and incidentally help to finance British and sterling area exports. Unless all governments were to agree to isolate their monetary systems from each other, this free market in money has come to stay. Isolation seems to be unlikely as this would lead to a collapse of international trade and the breakdown of international capital investments.

Central banks carry out their responsibility for the soundness and value of national currencies, but the currency in a modern state does not exist apart from the domestic and foreign banking systems, and no banking system in the western world can be treated in isolation from any other. Indeed, I am of the opinion that the western world now needs to move towards a common currency system, to avoid the damaging and, in the short run, useless movement of money across the international exchanges, blindly seeking the security of the soundest currency.

We also need to mobilise our capital resources through a comprehensive link-up between the main capital markets, and review the whole apparatus of the relations between domestic banks, foreign exchange markets and short term credit arrangements. London and New York possess the necessary expertise and banking structure on which the foundations of greater world-wide financial integration can be, and in fact are being, built—so that we can attempt to meet the demands for international credit and capital which seem to grow constantly.

The first world war destroyed the gold standard, the second the gold exchange standard and made paper money supreme. The cold war is tending to break down the differences between paper monies and to make all currencies issued by industrial countries very much alike; strength is a relative term, the reflection of weakness elsewhere. The inevitable direction of events is towards the unification of currency systems and the decline of national states. The best example of this tendency can be seen in the behaviour of the dollar and sterling which are now suffering from the international burden they carry. Pressure on sterling will ease as Britain's diminishing area of political power brings about a shrinkage of military responsibility.

The position I am moving towards is on the following lines:—

1. The American economic and therefore military potential is now probably fully exploited and, unless Washington reduces the military tempo, America will be caught in the scissors of growing strategic commitment and diminishing financial capacity. It is this dilemma that persuades Washington that some of the burden can be moved on to the shoulders of a unified western Europe which, it is naively believed, would finance without question American foreign policy.

2. Russia is being dragged unwillingly but inevitably into capitalist price and monetary systems, and must face the inherent contradictions between trade necessity and Marxist theory.

3. The Chinese enigma is beginning to resolve itself, and their age-old feeling of superiority over all other races is obviously playing a part in Sino-Russian relations. Russia expanded eastwards during the long period of Chinese weakness and she now has an immensely long border to defend. Peking overplayed its hand with the industrial "Great Leap Forward", but as soon as the Chinese develop industry and science, then Russia will be in danger and will seek support in the West.

4. America and Russia are being driven closer together and is it only proselytising "communism" that keeps them apart.
5. Western Europe still has to face further political decline, with the prospect, under current compulsions, of a Russian/American compromise over Berlin and the withdrawal of American ground forces from Germany.
6. The U.K. should now resign itself largely to a commerical and financial role internationally; our future lying in overseas development, particularly of Australia, New Zealand, India and North and South America.

Soon afterwards (1963) he added some further thoughts on the world situation in a talk to the Imperial Defence College. By this time his opposition to joining the European Common Market had hardened into hostility. He looked for a "Westerly instead of an Easterly emphasis" in British foreign and defence policies, and insisted that the national interest must in future be guided "by economic interest and by the reward of profits and capital development".

At the end of the last war those of us who had some knowledge of the financial background knew that our financial resources and economic structure were completely incapable of carrying the military burden. In 1945, when the post-war situation was being examined, the desperate position of the United Kingdom as the mother country of a political empire, and the centre of a large international financial apparatus emerged, and we found that the structure was hollow. It is difficult for me to say whether a conscious reappraisal of our political, economic and financial affairs was undertaken and that what has occurred since was part of a plan. But I have no hesitation in saying that it was a miracle that the sterling system survived, and an even greater miracle that the Commonwealth has been maintained in any recognisable form.

In 1946, we had over £4,000 million worth of sterling indebtedness due to countries, some of whom were in the sterling area and many of whom were not; and apart from manpower, we were without resources. We had to borrow $5,000 million, in 1946, from the United States and Canada in order to keep the economy going and help feed our people, and in addition we continued, wisely or unwisely, to accept a tremendous burden of international military responsibilities. If people of a logical cast of mind had been in charge of our affairs, even in spite of the Marshall Plan of 1948 they would undoubtedly have put us into both national and international bankruptcy.

As you are aware, this did not happen although the exchange crises of 1947 and 1949 showed how close we were to danger. The consequences of the last war have slowly been revealed to the people of this country, and this belated recognition has been accompanied by a great deal of anger and bewilderment, together with a wide spirit of personal denial of any form of responsibility. Much of what has occurred was probably inevitable, but it would have been more acceptable if it could have been absorbed over two or three generations instead of one.

This excursus is my attempt to introduce the subject of "national interest" and how it should be fostered and protected. In the past, the national interest was known to everybody in terms of imperial responsibilities. Apart from the entente cordiale, which now seems to have disappeared, and sporadic endeavours made to keep on terms with the American administrations, our international entanglements were few. We were a financial and military power in ourselves, supported in large part by the Indian Army and the subconscious loyalty to be found among the Australians, New Zealanders, South Africans and Canadians, and we needed, or so we thought, no permanent external supports. All this has now disappeared, and we are just one of many countries in NATO and SEATO; the Dominions have become independent national entities operating under their own conception of national interest. Our influence in Europe is not only very restricted, but has been challenged by the French on the grounds that it is non-existent. We remain in close association with various elements in the United States, but in no real position to influence American international policy.

My own experience and information lead me, therefore, to question the general assumptions about British national interest and the justification for vast and continuing military expenditure. In terms of military influence we are living on borrowed time, and hardly a day passes without our capacity to enforce foreign policy through the use of force being further diminished. I therefore come down on the economic side of the fence, namely that the national interest cannot escape in the future being guided by economic interest and by the reward of profits and capital development.

I would like to suggest that, in any reappraisal of national interest, defence policy should be related to foreign trade and finance. Relations with France will remain difficult, if not impossible, until there has been a major change of personalities and government. The Mediterranean is now a lake, with the eastern exit blocked and large parts of its shores under the control of nationalist regimes which appear to have recreated mediaeval conditions of personal and political insecurity. The oil bearing lands temporarily under our control are obviously of very great importance, but of less importance today than they were ten years ago. India, while it carries a substantial British investment, on the whole is a permanent source of weakness owing to the problems of population and living standards. We have considerable investments in Malaya, or the wider area called Malaysia, but I very much doubt whether they are worth great military expenditure. Hong Kong cannot be defended, and it survives only with the consent of mainland China. Yet I understand that we spend some £700 million annually for military purposes east of Suez. Africa, north of the Limpopo and with the exception of Nigeria, will be a source of political chaos and of financial pressure on our exiguous resources for which we will reap no economic return. South Africa remains in a kind of political limbo. Our national interest for the rest of this century in terms of my proposition will be centred not in the East but in:—

a) The economic ability and the financial resources of the British Isles, which are now recovering from the consequences of the wasted years of the twenties, thirties and forties; economic associations with Europe are important in this context.
b) Our business and family and cultural associations with Australia, New Zealand, Canada and the United States, and
c) South America, the great sub-continent, the only area rich in all that the world has to offer to mankind and which is still an unexploited continent; more important, it is without any defined political affiliations.

There is a general disposition to believe that Latin America is the home of revolution, monetary chaos and a feudal social structure where the rich get richer and the poor poorer. There is some truth in this generalisation but, in reality, a closer contact with the various countries produces a very different reaction. For more than a generation now, Mexico has, under a form of government of her own devising, maintained political stability. The democratic credentials of Uruguay are unimpeachable. Indeed, throughout most of the continent, whatever may be said about the gap between theory and practice of democracy, there is a genuine regard for personal liberties and freedom of the press that does not exist, even as an aspiration, in many parts of the world. What is also remarkable is the relatively small success, where freedom of choice is allowed, of extremist movements of the Left and the lack of evidence in Latin America, as elsewhere in the world, that Communism can come to power except in the wake of civil war. And, although Cuba remains a centre of subversion, the United States by her forthright action in October 1962 has prevented what might otherwise have led to a collapse of her position in the Western hemisphere.

At a time when the neutralist, anti-colonialist, or even frankly hostile, attitudes of Africa and Asia receive sympathetic consideration from observers in Europe, there has been little attempt to understand Latin America and its problems, or to offer more than recipes based on generalisation from North American and European experience. Except by the relatively few students of Latin American history, it is not generally understood that the revolutions in Spanish-speaking America were organised at the top and that basically the Army, and in some cases the Navy, became in default of any political organisation the sole source of law and order. The social conditions of the countries remained relatively unchanged throughout the nineteenth century; the political parties were at their best embryonic, and in few countries were the intelligent and patriotic elements attracted into politics.

The decision to rivet on to this feeble structure a system of government that was basically Northern European in origin, Protestant in outlook, and dependent upon an efficient and incorruptible Civil Service, has been in many respects a fatal mistake. The most helpful policy of the American and Western European governments would be to adopt a more benevolent attitude towards the various political adventures undertaken by these countries, and to refrain from assuming that their own forms of government are divinely inspired.

I will now return to "national interest". If there is any possibility of the future international policy of Great Britain having a Westerly instead of an Easterly emphasis, it will be unsuccessful unless our econmic and political links with the leading South American countries are reforged. If one were to assume, for example, that we should, like Christopher Columbus, approach India from the west instead of the east, our lines of communication must pass through Canada, the Pacific Islands and Australia. If we regard Australia, as I do, as perhaps our major long term national interest, it would be essential to have alternative lines of communication. We should, therefore, build up good relations with the temperate zone, viz. Argentina, Chile and Uruguay, and develop close political and economic relations. It will be very important that the air routes over Antarctica and Patagonia to Australia should be organised without fear of international complications. The financial, political and defence complex needs very careful examination, as it requires a comprehensive association with Argentina and Chile, and a resolution between ourselves and Argentina over the Falkland Islands dependencies dispute. It involves a deliberate movement by industry in this country, sponsored and fostered by HMG, to assist in the growth of the industralisation of the Southern half of the Latin American continent—Uruguay, Argentina and Chile.

When the negotiations for British entry into the E.E.C. broke down under President de Gaulle's first veto in January 1963, Bolton's doubts grew stronger, and he became entirely hostile to any renewal of the attempt. There was more than injured pride in this reaction. In his view the Cuba missile crisis of October 1962 made any future war between the United States and the Soviet Union unthinkable, and he took it for granted that the two super-powers would now explore the possibilities of peaceful co-operation. This, he argued, changed the role of Europe in the world and made the idea of a Western European block look both less essential and too restrictive.

A lively sketch of this argument was produced in a speech in June 1964:

I believe it to be well known among my close friends that I was critical of the policy of seeking to enter the Common Market. This was not because I was opposed to any movement towards the unification of Europe, but largely because I felt the move was badly timed and would inevitably fail. There were also other considerations which have become a little clearer since the Brussels fiasco, and I would like to mention them briefly.

First, I believe we are now in a political condition known as "peace", I am convinced that, while the Bomb is available, we are never likely again to experience a world war. One consequence will be that the pressures that forced Europe together will now diminish and the inherent frictions will again emerge. Second, the Communist system cannot provide enough food or consumer goods for more that a permanent policy of austerity; it can now be established that the socialist system of management is dependent on the western world for marginal food and consumer requirements of the community. The survival of Communist forms of government will therefore depend upon the continued growth of the Western system of agriculture, trade and finance. Marxism has been defeated on grounds of its own choosing.

Third, we are now moving into a cycle where the immediate post-war fears of commodity shortages may have relevance; the terms of trade, which since the Korean war have been heavily weighted in favour of the industrialised countries, are beginning to favour the primary producers, and this movement will gather momentum if, as I fear, much of Africa becomes incapable of achieving export surpluses. Finally—and this is perhaps the most important consideration—the United States is becoming immersed in domestic problems and is finding her role as the leader of the western world more onerous than it has ever been since the end of the war. They have had to deal with the problem of a weakened exchange position at a time when they were carrying—as they still do—a heavy overseas military burden and an immense foreign aid programme. If Washington is forced to look inwards when it is already disenchanted with foreign aid and the behaviour of its allies, American foreign policy may change overnight.

These are the elements which lead me to believe that, if a lasting unification of Europe is to be achieved, we should take into account first the probability that Russia and the Eastern European countries generally described as satellites will be gradually subsumed into the comity of Europe. Any development of this nature will expose the Six members of the Common Market to marked changes in both political and economic policies and a reassessment of their objectives. I suggest that, if general European unity is to be achieved, it should begin not at the political level but at a lower level, for example public services. I see no reason why there should not be a European railway system, a merger of the European air lines, an Electricity Board co-ordinating all electricity generation and distribution throughout Europe; similarly a European Gas Board and, perhaps in time, a European capital market with agreed rules and procedures. In all these activities, Britain would I am sure play her part and a movement towards political unity could be built up on firmer foundations.

Assumptions and possibilities of this kind affect Britain's future policies and our national interests. Our traditional spheres of influence in Africa and the Middle East are being rapidly eroded and our traditional eastward lines of communication are in jeopardy. It is, I believe, essential that we should henceforth think in continental terms, starting with Europe which must include European Russia.

I therefore come to the conclusions that our foreign policy and economic policy for the rest of this century should revolve round the maintenance of the closest possible relations with Australia and Canada, the United States and the whole of Europe; and that we should concentrate on trading and financial relations with these areas. The West, under the leadership of the United States, has won the cold war; the final and decisive battle was the confrontation over Cuba in October 1962, although Russia had already lost the war on the economic front. The only difficulty is to be found in the United States, where there appears to be little or no recognition of the fact that she and her allies have won a great and lasting victory.

A month later he developed his ideas for a fresh start in British foreign policy more fully in another talk to the Imperial Defence College, enlarging on his view that the West had won the cold war against Soviet Russia.

It is exactly a year to the day when I spoke to this gathering on the theme of our wasteful expenditure on eastward lines of communication and the necessity to examine the westward alternative. I now propose to reappraise this theme in relation to some recent developments. The political and strategic history of the post-war period can be briefly summed up: the development of an apparently monolithic Communist block as a major world power under the leadership of Russia, and the West's counteraction based on the Dulles strategy of containment and encirclement leading to the current stalemate.

We have seen the underdeveloped Afro-Asian nations multiplying as they gain independence, to the point where they are able to outvote the major powers in the innumerable world organisations; we also have the spectacle of the Communist bloc breaking apart on the doctrinal quarrel between the U.S.S.R. and China, kept carefully concealed for many years but now completely in the open, and with a consequential weakening of the Russian domination of Eastern Europe.

The most important development, however, and one which may affect politics and philosophy for the next generation, is the failure of the Communist system in the sphere basic to its philosophy—that is in economic planning. The most publicised example of this is the present Russian and Chinese dependence on the West for food grains and modern industrial plants.

China's aggressive nationalism is spurred by the population increase and the present total of 700 million is growing at a rate of between twelve and fifteen million per annum. Much of China consists of uninhabitable desert or mountains, and expansion of living space can only be achieved at the expense of Russia or India. It is obvious that Russia realises this, and is especially susceptible as her imperial expansion into Asia is historically very recent. Much of Russian territorial gains are less than a hundred years old and almost entirely at the expense of the old imperial China enshrined in treaties now publicly regarded by modern China as examples of aggressive imperialism.

Russia politically and economically is therefore being impelled to move, however reluctantly, towards a composition with the West. The Communist theologians find this incompatible with the Marxist gospel and Russia will thus move forward erratically into closer connections with the West, making practical arrangements to meet current emergencies, e.g., food and fertilisers, while still proselitising in Cuba, Zanzibar, Algeria, etc.

Unfortunately, while Western Europe is becoming conditioned for better relations with Russia, the United States remains the capitve of post-war attitudes and slogans and a foreign policy based fundamentally on the unification of Germany and the restoration of the Nationalist government of China, both totally unrealistic objectives but identified with the policy of resisting communism.

During the last months of President Kennedy's life, the Government of the United States had begun to grind to a halt, due to an overloaded programme and the controversial Civil Rights issue. While liberal minded people feel it is fundamentally wrong that black and white should not live side by side as equals, we cannot neglect evidence on all sides that the less literate and less sophisticated mass of the white population react violently against this philosophy. In view of the traditional and emotional reaction of the white masses in the north as well as in the south, there are dangerous possibilities. I would suggest that there is sufficient evidence available to convince interested observers that both Russian and American foreign policies are ripe for a change.

I have little to say about British policy which is a closed book to the ordinary public; we seem to be engaged with remnants of strategies and tactics inherited from the 1930's. For example, we appear to view defence from two different and inconsistent points of view: our national interests and out international commitments. The Navy, for example, no longer exists to protect British commerical interests abroad; membership of the United Nations makes this impossible. HMG gives political primacy to Anglo/American relations and the NATO commitments and, in the dispostion of our forces, priority has been given to the discouragement of potential Communist aggression by membership of NATO, SEATO, CENTO and so on.

Much attention is concentrated on the problems arising from the fricitions in Cyprus, Aden, North Borneo, Indo-China, Formosa, Korea, Congo, etc. But all these incidents are part of the pattern arising directly either from the consequences of the Dulles containment policy, or from the withdrawal of Europe from the responsibility of maintaining law and order in Africa, Asia and the Middle East. They attract much public attention but have no long run importance. Unfortunately, they distract attention from the areas where vital decisions are emerging or being made by default: Western Europe and Latin America.

Western Europe has passed through the stage of economic expansion and is faced by internal social and political problems. Personal dictatorships exist in Portugal, Spain, France and, apart from the United Kingdom, Scandinavia and the Netherlands, parliamentary democracy is everywhere on the defensive. Italy cannot produce a stable elected government and is rapidly moving towards the only alternative, a new dictatorship. The argument about Britain joining or not joining the Common Market is only of ephemeral importance; what has real significance is the relationship which must be organised between Russia and Western Europe.

Latin America is significant in these complicated relationships. I have little doubt that Russia hoped both to spread friendly communist dictatorships and to outflank the United States in this subcontinent through a base in Cuba and the effective control of Brazil. Two dates are extremely important. The 16th October 1962, when Khruschev retreated from Cuba against the threat of nuclear war, leaving Castro with nothing much more than nuisance value as a centre of local subversion. And the 31st March 1964, when Goulart and his Left Wing administration were expelled from Brazil with popular acclamation. Any hopes that Moscow might have had of weighting the strategic scales against the United States by a major distraction in South America and the Caribbean have had to be abandoned for the time being. Russia is left with two basic problems: appeasement of the Russian public who expect results from the regime, and the defence of their vulnerable Eastern Marches. It will be interesting to see whether HMG and the other European governments take advantage of the various opportunities now becoming negotiable.

I come to the conclusion that our foreign policy for the rest of this century should revolve round the maintenance of the closest possible ties and the development of trading and financial relations with Western Europe and Latin America; also with the older white dominions, the United States and Russia.

THE BREAK-UP OF THE STERLING SYSTEM

The year 1964 was a critical period for the policies which Bolton had advocated since the end of the war. He himself would place the beginning of the great British decline about ten years earlier—more precisely with the defeat of the "Butler policies" of 1952 which were to have made the pound convertible, relaxed and finally lifted exchange controls, and exposed the economy to the cold winds of competition. Many of his friends must have heard him deplore the rejection of these policies "by a group of tired old men without imagination" as a historic error, from which, as he saw it, flowed the disasters and demoralisation of the sixties. Whether historians of the period will accept this sequence is open to debate; few economists will see it in that way, and one may be sure that Bolton would be quite unmoved by their arguments.

In 1964, at any rate, other chickens besides the decisions of 1952 were coming home to roost. The defeat at Suez was still being paid for in expensive confusions of foreign policy. Economic policy at home was bedevilled by the Radcliffe Report of 1959 which led to a neglect of monetary control. Any remaining chance of preserving something of the sterling system was probably thrown away in 1962 when Prime Minister Harold Macmillan dismissed Selwyn Lloyd as Chancellor and put in Reginald Maudling with a mandate to accelerate economic growth. Plans were laid almost at once for further large increases in government expenditure. The hope that the external payments deficit resulting from internal expansion would soon be corrected by the impact of faster growth on industrial vigour and productivity proved to be illusory, at any rate in the time-span left until the reserves and borrowing facilities ran out.

In the course of 1964 the payments deficit grew alarmingly large, too large to be bridged by the credit arrangement Maudling had made for the purpose. For a time the mass of new pounds put into foreign hands by the U.K. deficit stayed in London, where interest rates were very high and the money market had developed an unheard-of sophistication. A few weeks before the October elections, overseas sterling deposits in London reached almost an all-time record, and there was remarkably little forward covering of exchange risks.

Then came the Labour government, a crisis of confidence, a panic flight from sterling, and a short term credit of $3,000 million raised by Lord Cromer, then Governor of the Bank of England, from foreign central banks. The writing was on the wall. After one more attempt in 1965 to "plan" for expansion and hope that external balance would follow in time, the growth policy collapsed in 1966, but not before further large short term debts had been incurred abroad to keep the pound afloat. In his annual review for the year 1965 Bolton drew a fresh picture of Britain's precarious position in the world, stressing the remaining strength of the "financial, industrial and technical resources" which might still form a viable foundation "if they were not wastefully deployed in sterile policies."

A realistic appraisal of Britain's potential and weaknesses must lead to the conclusion that the country no longer possesses the resources to behave like a world power—accepting costly military and development aid obligations in the areas of the Mediterranean, Indian Ocean and the China Seas, and generally in Africa and South East Asia—and at the same time to act as banker to the sterling area, finance a large part of the world's trade, provide an effective capital market, and maintain at home a rising standard of living together with expensive social services.

It must be recognised that Britain's reserves, resources, balance of payments and export earnings were damaged—it seems almost irreparably—by the second world war and its strategic and financial repercussions. The negligible international reserves that Britain now owns, as distinct from those that are borrowed, have been shown on more than one occasion in recent years to be inadequate to support the sterling area and military commitments abroad, provide economic aid to the Commonwealth countries, counter speculative moves against sterling, and permit an adequate level of overseas investment. In an economy which, if not declining, is at the best static there is an urgent need for a reconsideration of priorities in the use or our totally inadequate economic resources.

The frequent exhortations to British industry to improve its export performance are related to the balance of payments and its component factors, yet it must be evident that physical exports and invisible earnings are unlikely ever to finance all the country's current foreign expenditure, including an adequate level of imports of food and raw materials. A proper assessment of priorities should recognise that imports are vital; Britain does not produce enough food for its own survival, nor all the raw materials needed for the maintenance of industrial activity. Not nearly enough attention has been paid to the sources of these essential supplies, nor to the dangers to Britain implicit in the growth of the world population and consumption of food and raw materials in relation to comparatively stagnant production. It is short-sighted to assume that the only factor now governing Britain's supplies is the ability to pay. The strength that this country once derived from being the world's largest importer is now in danger of becoming a serious weakness.

Sentiment, or simply habits of thought, have led Britain to maintain military, political and financial connections with regions that are politically unstable and commercially of little interest. Government policies, to be effective, require the co-operation of the private sector, yet the current political climate in the greater part of Africa and the East—towards which British policy still maintains a complacent, indeed a euphoric, attitude—hardly makes for attractive investment and trading prospects. I remain convinced that Britain's long-term interests are mainly in Australasia, the Western Hemisphere and Europe. The concept of Britain as the centre of a vast multi-racial Commonwealth has outlived the existence of the Commonwealth itself, which no longer has real cohesion, responds to no central idea and is disintegrating. This is plainly displayed, for example, in the boundary problems of India and Pakistan where Britain has been quietly displaced by the U.S.S.R.

Australia, New Zealand and Canada are of vital interest to Britain, not merely because they are well disposed towards the continuing British connection or because they are the "old dominions", but because they are important sources of essential supplies, they are economically viable and politically stable, and they are rewarding partners in trade and investment. Australia deserves particular attention as an under-populated land mass in the shadow of a chaotic Indonesia and an aggressive land-hungry China; the development, industrialisation and effective peopling of Western Australia should be an aim of high priority, for both economic and strategic reasons. Canada is of special importance by reason of its situation in the Western Hemisphere, its close commercial and financial links with the U.S.A., with which Britain also has particular ties, and its permanent export capacity in grains and minerals.

Apart from long-standing political connections, which cannot be discounted even by critics of U.S. policies in other parts of the world, the financial and monetary interdependence of Britain and the U.S.A. is by itself sufficient reason for maintaining the closest possible alliance. The sterling and dollar systems depend largely on each other, if for no other reason than the dependence of the capitalist world on the comprehensive market facilities offered by New York and London. Large amounts of British and U.S. capital are involved in industrial ventures in each other's countries, and Britain depends on many products of U.S. origin. There is no doubt that closer British collaboration with the two English-speaking North American nations in promoting the expansion of developing countries would be more effective than independent efforts and pointless rivalry. This concept underlies this Bank's recent association with the Mellon National Bank & Trust Company of Pittsburgh, and its earlier connection with the Bank of Montreal in the creation of the subsidiary Bank of London & Montreal; these are practical expressions of the firm belief that Britain's future is closely linked with North America.

Besides Britain's need to concentrate its financial, technical and diplomatic resources in the Western Hemisphere and Australasia, it is also important that Britain should recognise that these islands are economically, historically and racially part of Europe. Some awareness of the point was shown with the formation of the European Free Trade Association (EFTA) and in 1962 when Britain tried to negotiate its entry into the European Economic Community (EEC). The fact that these negotiations failed did not alter Britain's geographical position, but demonstrated that partnership in a community still dominated by nationalism, especially the Gaullist variety, was not yet a possibility.

The same nationalism has more recently come near to paralysing the EEC, and it is by no means certain that the Community will recover its initial vigour while French policy is in conflict with that of the other five members. The EEC was originally the creation of a few brilliant men who saw that a postwar Europe of seventeen nations and almost as many cultures and languages was historically unstable and needed a unifying ethos; the effort to unite the countries that represented the power centres of two world wars was largely successful, but the EEC is not representative of Europe as a whole. Statistically the Six represent less than two-thirds of the total gross domestic product of Western Europe, and only half the population; politically the EEC is inward-looking and self-protective; commercially it gives too little attention to the needs of the developing world.

While the Community retains these characteristics, Britain could not be a member without endangering its world trade and in particular the provenance of food and raw materials. A wider community is needed if the integration of Western Europe is to become a dynamic movement in keeping with the underlying philosophy of the Treaty of Rome. The economic policies of such a community should be outward-looking rather than protective. The eventual inclusion of the countries of Eastern Europe, though at present involving larger problems, should not be ignored as a long term objective to be attained with the lessening of cold war tensions.

European integration will not become a reality until every country's policy, including Britain's, encourages international mergers of industrial and financial institutions. It is already noticeable that the operations of some of the very large international companies are too big for individual parochial banking systems; banking integration must accompany the necessary industrial integration. It is obvious that the financial basis for European integration cannot be limited to the narrow confines of the Six; for example, any viable financial system must include Switzerland as well as Britain.

Britain could play an important role in such a community; the weakest aspect of the EEC is in the financial sphere, where it is noticeable that the European systems have been slow to respond to the opportunities afforded them by the restraints imposed on London and New York as financial centres. For some years to come, there is no real substitute in Europe for the mechanism and expertise of the London market. British policy towards Europe should not be confined to another attempt to become an incompatible partner with the Six, nor to attempt to build tenuous bridges between the EEC and the EFTA; policy should rather give freedom to industrial and banking interests pragmatically to pursue the European idea without political commitment. It is of vital importance that Britain, as a major industrial country, should have access to this high income market of some 200 million people.

Britain also has old and valuable, though somewhat neglected, connections with the republics of Latin America, particularly Argentina, Brazil, Chile, Peru and Uruguay. There are historical reasons, beginning with the world slump of the thirties, for the comparative neglect of South America by all but a few private companies and a handful of enthusiastic government officials and academics. But today there is no longer any justification for this neglect.

The Latin American republics have already emerged as politically and economically mature nations with stable governments, in contrast to Africa and the East where the process of growing up is in its very early stages. This is not to say that the irruption of the cold war into Latin America can be ignored. Since the Cuban crisis, the threat of Communist subversion in any Latin American republic is taken much more seriously; the region is no longer regarded by the U.S.A. as a safe area. Some Latin American governments may be to the left of centre, but most are firmly anti-Communist and should be clearly distinguished from the vociferous and sometimes violent extremists. Movements for reform are skilfully combining nationalism—to satisfy the aim of avoiding political and economic domination by the U.S.A.—with a committed position as nations with European traditions and culture essentially friendly to the U.S.A. and Western Europe. Once it is accepted that the social and agrarian reforms on which they are determined call for policies that place them farther to the left than United States political sentiment, it will be seen that it is governments of this kind that are most likely to co-operate with the U.S.A. by pursuing the aims of the Alliance for Progress. It is important that every assistance should be given to these reform movements and that nothing should check the promising political trend.

The Alliance for Progress is, almost imperceptibly perhaps, developing political stability in Latin America and, as its original concepts are modified, helping politically mature forces to emerge. Neither the Latin Americans themselves, nor the U.S.A., regard Latin America as a United States preserve, and there is no reason why Britain should do so. Britain's interests in Australasia and North America, seen against the troubled areas to the east of the Atlantic, suggest quite clearly the need for disinvolvement from fruitless and financially wasteful commitments and a redirection of Britain's efforts, resources and communications westwards. The whole of the Western Hemisphere, an area essentially friendly and welcoming British collaboration, faces Australasia across the Pacific, which could become as important a trade route as the Atlantic is today, especially when a second canal is cut through the Isthmus of Central America.

Britain's financial, industrial and technical resources are considerable and, if they were not wastefully deployed in sterile policies, could be a fruitful contribution to the development, prosperity and commerce of the great regions that are Britain's most rewarding partners.

> Everything seemed to go wrong in 1966, and the exchange crisis of July which led to the abandonment of the "National Plan" and an attempt to freeze wages was not followed by any new policies that might have inspired new hope. Bolton did not find it easy, in reviewing the events of that year, to look into the future with any confidence. He found the task "complex and challenging" but outlined some of the more promising events.

The year 1966 was exceedingly troubled; hardly any continent escaped political disturbances, one of the consequences of which has been a growing economic malaise affecting one country after another. The United Kingdom has been particularly disturbed by these events, and a weak sterling exchange position has been exacerbated by domestic and foreign policies that have helped to increase the pressures against sterling. A growing deterioration in our affairs culminated in the drastic deflationary measures against the private sector introduced by the Government on 20th July 1966. The immediate sterling crisis seems to be over, but the foreign exchange aspect of our affairs continues to be depressed by heavy military expenditure abroad and the growing demands of government and municipalities on the country's capital resources, leaving inadequate funds to sustain industry. There seems to be little possibility of this situation changing in 1967, and we may be approaching something in the nature of a siege economy.

In such circumstances the task of an international banking organisation is both complex and challenging; our activities in the United Kingdom, in which we have experienced the same difficulties as other institutions in the City, our interests in the U.S.A. and continental Europe, and our large domestic operations in Latin America, have all been directly or indirectly affected by the major political and economic disturbances of the world. This has meant a constant adjustment of details of policy within the general principles under which we operate as an overseas bank, and an unrelenting search for lines of activity that could profitably be developed in changing circumstances and despite new difficulties.

The military situation in the Far East is increasingly affecting world monetary and economic affairs and in particular the U.S. balance of payments, which has tended to become a catalyst accelerating enquiry into world liquidity and the place of gold in the international payments system. Unless the war in Vietnam ceases, the distortions created by the uncertain international supply of dollars aggravated by the adoption of restrictive measures by Washington, approximating to exchange control, will make it hard to avoid further difficulties in international payments.

In the years of large U.S. deficits, creditors were to a large extent willing to hold dollars—claims on the U.S. Treasury—instead of demanding payment in gold; in 1965, however, the reduced deficit was largely settled in gold, with the result that no new cash assets were created; the same is probably true for 1966. The question of world liquidity or the total of international reserves has therefore acquired a more urgent significance, and the deliberations of the Group of Ten and the International Monetary Fund are being more closely followed.

The Group of Ten has made some progress in its search for common ground that would enable it to introduce a contingency plan for the creation of additional reserve assets. The sort of scheme that is being sought would have the advantage that, unlike a general revaluation of gold, it would enable new assets to be created in the volume required and at the moment when they were needed; such a plan would allow for regulation of the total of assets without giving any advantage to particular countries. Provided that this creation of international paper money were in technical hands and were not subject to the obvious dangers of political pressures, it would have the advantage of reducing the role of gold, which is today no more than a crude monetary regulator, but which may become of greater industrial importance in the long run.

Alone among the Ten, the French authorities consider contingency planning to be premature. Their contention is that there is no real shortage of international liquidity and that the creation of new assets would only accentuate the existing threat of inflation. The other members of the Group believe, however, that with the elimination of the payments deficits of the two reserve currency countries, international reserves will cease to expand at an adequate rate, and that this could make the problems of international payments more difficult for the developing countries than it is already.

The difference of view would appear to arise, political considerations apart, from the assumption inherent in the French view that balances of payments consist only of movements in current account. The present state of reserve assets, while it may be adequate for current account movements, leaves little margin for international capital movements and investment; this is perhaps one of the weakest features of the existing international structure which is acting as an impediment to the expansion of the developing countries. If additional reserves enable the rich nations to play a larger part in the capital expansion of the developing countries, such a plan would be amply justified; indeed, there may be a case for aiming it at this objective.

The immense changes since 1945 in the world role of Britain and in our financial situation, where the British Government is in danger of becoming a permanent debtor dependent on the goodwill of its creditors, make it difficult for the ordinary citizen to realise that from a world point of view his opinions and aspirations now carry little weight. In the new circumstances, the international banking and other services provided by the United Kingdom represent a world influence of singular importance; and yet our fiscal and economic policy appears to be based on the fallacy that only the work of men's hands is useful and saleable, while the output of applied and disciplined intelligence is of little value.

Social policy, with its emphasis on comprehensive education and far wider opportunities for the cultivation of the intelligent student, is incompatible with economic and fiscal policies that stress the overriding importance of the role of the manual worker, and tend to make fresh initiative by aspirants seeking personal responsibility not worth while. This is all the more irrational when technical developments are responsible for the growing redundancy of the weekly wage earner in both factory and office. If, as a consequence of fiscal and social legislation, the international services sold by this country were to diminish or even emigrate to a more hospitable climate, then the "brains" trained at great cost would also have to emigrate.

There is a need for the reconciliation of the vital importance of Britain's external activities with the problem of short term pressures on the balance of payments. There is no real doubt that overseas investments and credits are not only direct earners of foreign exchange, but are also an important indirect influence in promoting exports; they also have some influence on invisible exports derived from trade. Australia and the Latin American countries, for example, are all on the point of major expansion and politically are oases of stability compared with many other regions. They will continue to need foreign capital in one form or another for many years but as their economies expand and overcome the distortions and instabilities of transition, they will become increasingly rewarding partners with which to be associated in trade and development.

Most of the problems here commented upon are not only reacting on each other, but they all affect overseas bankers who have to cope with all current difficulties of political or monetary origin, maintain an organisation and make a net profit. United States and British military expenditure is directly responsible for the weakness of the dollar and sterling, high rates of interest, and the reduced flow of capital to developing countries. This will continue until more peaceful relations develop between the West and the Russian and Chinese spheres of influence. The foreign policy of the EEC, under French influence, seems to be based on an attempt to isolate Western Europe from these quarrels and to organise an economic and political policy wholly "European". This is an understandable but illusory hope; but while the effort continues the position of the raw material and food producers will be further damaged; population growth will continue practically unchecked and the longer term need for enlarged food resources will be forgotten. The countries of the western world need to be less self-regarding and should examine long-term policies to safeguard their future by encouraging the growth of the developing areas of the world. Such policies would be not only economically but also politically wise, as wealth and poverty cannot exist together for long without approaching explosion point. So far as Britain is concerned, every effort should be made to modernise her industry and rebuild her overseas connections involved in the exploitation and expansion of food and mineral production. Her people have, over the years, shown their genius in these fields; despite the recent neglect of her friends overseas and despite the atmosphere of frustration under which she is labouring, she should now set herself to the constructive development of her overseas heritage, to the benefit of all.

Continuing the inquest on the exchange crisis of 1966 he spoke to the Economic Research Council in December on "The Problem of the Exchanges", pleading rather surprisingly for "the survival of the sterling area without which the standard of living of this country will rapidly decline".

The foreign exchange markets are now much more difficult to understand than they were in the days of metallic standards, whether based on silver or gold, when textbooks could be written based on consistent experience. But the gold standard finally expired in 1933, when America went off gold and President Roosevelt and Mr. Morgenthau decided to fix the price of gold from day to day on the toss of a coin. The silver standard, which had prevailed in the Far East for centuries, finally collapsed when the American advisers to the Kuomintang recommended the issue of a paper currency and the withdrawal of silver from circulation. I personally date the triumph of Communism in China from this unfortunate recommendation. However, let us leave silver out of this discussion, although from an industrial point of view it is now a far more important metal than gold and is probably in permanent short supply. The final breakdown of the gold standard in the thirties, followed by the second world war, brought about the current regimen for paper money which has progressively become the sole means of financial communication between countries and of financing foreign trade. Since the thirties, the phrase "key currency" has been taken up by economists and the press; much of the controversy that rages over the incapacity of this country to sustain the sterling system, as well as the current criticism of the dollar system, arises from the fact that there is no non-political money, such as a metal, available to the trading world, although international settlements between central banks are still made in gold and private gold hoarding continues on an extensive scale.

There are numerous descriptions of the nature, character and purpose of paper money, many of which have been borrowed from the experience of bankers, traders and economic students of a world which ultimately settled its balances in a metal. I have spent nearly fifty years in the financial field, of which well over thirty have been connected with the activities of the Bank of England. During this period, I have not been able to discover any satisfactory explanation of the character and behaviour of paper money. The reason is, I believe, that paper money in itself has no intrinsic value. It is not something that can be weighed, measured and assayed like a metal with a world wide value. It is not a concrete thing; it is merely an abstraction, and, what is worse, now that the issue of paper money is almost entirely in the hands of governments, it is a political abstraction. Its value depends to some extent on scarcity, but fundamentally on the belief of a people in its government and institutions, and a conviction by the people that their country and its financial system will survive. All this is summed up in the word confidence, but few endeavour to define precisely what is meant by confidence. In spite of differences of language, printing, denomination and issue, all paper monies are much the same and behave according to the same set of rules. I would not pretend to be able to set out the rules in order of priority, but they include:–

1. The level of government expenditure, whether or not financed by taxation; once government expenditure brings about a level of taxation that acts as a disincentive to effort, then what is called the "confidence factor" begins to operate. If government expenditure is financed by the printing presses, then confidence evaporates more quickly.
2. As soon as a country appears to be weak and divided and poor

relative to other countries, irrespective of monetary policy, the "confidence factor" intervenes.

3. If a country develops a political philosophy based on say religious principles in a world where these principles do not universally apply, then that country will, rightly or wrongly, begin to decline. In a world of material values, moral attitudes tend to have an unfortunate influence on economics. These may be unfamiliar concepts to people considering monetary and exchange policies, but they apply from time to time to any country.

One of the monetary situations inherited from the interregnum between the two world wars is the consequence of national sovereignty. In the nineteenth century, there was basically one international currency, gold coins, in spite of the bi-metallic controversy and the rise of the nation state. There were also a number of international financial centres, London, New York, Paris and Berlin, with a monopoly of finance for trade, domestic and international, and of the provision of long term capital for development. National boundaries, although they had a profound significance from a political and military point of view, had practically no effect on financial decisions. Once paper currency, issued by national authorities, prevailed, then the universal monetary system began to break down; self-regarding political parties claimed that the control of the central bank, exchanges, prices and wages, etc., enabled them to provide a better living for the ordinary man.

The greatest hopes for future stability are to be placed on the efforts of the Group of Ten, who are endeavouring to convert the active co-operation of the central banks into something more schematic and less dependent upon individual national decisions. There is no doubt of the devoted services of this small group of men to a world which barely knows of their existence and certainly does not know any of their names. Although there are many currencies and countries involved in current controversies, there is time only to make a brief reference to the United States, the United Kingdom and gold.

It is axiomatic that the sheer size of the American economy is such that its state of health can have a marked influence on international financial affairs, through internal as well as external pressures on the dollar, on the stock markets of the major trading nations of the western hemisphere and on commodity price levels. Those involved in the daily movement of money across the exchanges of the world need to be aware of the influences liable to affect the normal trading positions. To be able to anticipate the movement of exchange and interest rates, in so far as this is ever possible, requires an appreciation of the major political and economic issues in the United States. Because of the current importance of the U.S. dollar as the main channel of communication and calculation between other currencies, it is interesting to examine briefly the political, monetary and banking situations in North America.

One of the major causes of the disturbed conditions in the international exchanges over the past two years has been the general unwillingness of governments to employ fiscal measures against increasingly obvious symptoms of "over-heating". The decision earlier this year by President Johnson not to ask Congress for an increase in taxation started a chain of events which might well have been avoided if political necessities had not overruled other considerations. As a result of a credit squeeze by the Federal Reserve which coincided with a massive run off of certificates of deposit following a restriction on the rate of interest to be paid by the banks, many American banks were at the point where they could not meet their customers' normal requirements. The second line of reserves disappeared as government and municipal bonds became progressively unsaleable. American banks' offices in Europe were instructed to bid any price for money in order to assist their head offices' cash positions and this, combined with the excessive use of monetary restrictions not only in the United States but in Germany as well, helped to bring about the July/August run on sterling. The panic subsided following the reminder by the FRB of the existence of rediscounting facilities and a statement from President Johnson that he would not rely on monetary measures alone to control inflation. Unless either tax increases are introduced next year or the Vietnam war expenditure is significantly reduced or there is a substantial turndown in business, the tight money situation in the United States will continue to bedevil European exchanges and stock markets.

I now turn to sterling. Our sterling area heritage lays us open to the critical scrutiny of the world's bankers and what they have seen over the past two years has scarcely reassured them. Successive sterling crises are an eloquent if painful reminder of their disapproval. But the root of the problem is not as easy to define as many would like to think. It is easy enough to lay the blame at the door of our exporters who are chided for failing in their task of balancing our trading account. But this is not the whole story. The problem is more a combination of factors; a legacy of the immediate postwar apathy which settled over Britain in the wake of six years of unprecedented national effort. It was only recently, after the door to Europe was so abruptly slammed in our faces, that a general reappraisal of Britain's future indicated that the country could simply not afford to live in the past. Our weaknesses are obvious; an overstrained domestic economy following an attempt to expand social services and Commonwealth development programmes and to raise the standard of living without regard to capital resources. The situation has been exacerbated by the load of military expenditure, which is partly an imperial inheritance, partly the consequence of commitment in international bodies, such as NATO, CENTO, SEATO and partly an inability to avoid involvement in overseas expenditure. The facts today are that we maintain a precarious international foreign policy, the financial consequences of which we cannot support; it follows that our trade and international services are in grave danger unless there are some decisive changes in policy; and it is precisely these which we have not seen. The Rhodesian conflict is a particular example of our difficulties.

The muddled Government planning of the past years has been largely responsible for the long agony of sterling. While government and local authority expenditure continued to rise to the extent that capital investment urgently required by industry was being gradually stifled, foreign holders of sterling were simply not prepared to listen to the Government's protestations of good intent. It has required a series of stringent deflationary measures and considerable discomfort to the British people before a glimmer of light has become perceptible.

What now seems to be emerging as a pattern for the future is a tightly controlled wages and prices policy at least until the British balance of payments is seen to be moving into surplus. It is to be hoped that the tight controls against sterling area borrowing will be relaxed, if only to assure the survival of the sterling area, without which the standard of living of this country will rapidly decline.

I have mentioned the psychological problems associated with paper money and some of the current problems affecting the sterling and dollar exchanges, and I have implied that they can only be dealt with on a pragmatic basis. The various questions regarding the role of gold in international payments, the price of gold and attempts made by the leading central banks to provide a permanent alternative to gold, all help to keep the exchanges in a ferment. It should, I believe, be clear to everyone that gold in the western world is a subject only of debate between governments and central banks, as the ordinary man now has no contact with gold coinage which started to go out of circulation some fifty years ago. In these circumstances, gold remains important while national sovereignty prevails and national governments distrust each other. There are of course very large private holdings of gold representing capital resources which have been withdrawn from circulation. But large as the total gold hoarding appears to be, it represents a drop in the ocean compared with capital values expressed in national currencies. In the long run, gold is likely to retain its usefulness in the eastern countries where there is a long tradition of political instability, social inequality and total distrust of governments and politicians. But in Europe, East and West, in the sterling area generally and in the Americas it would seem probable that eventually a universal paper currency system will emerge organised by the central banks, the International Monetary Fund and the Bank for International Settlements.

But this will take time and we must expect the present confusion to continue until governments realise the limitation on national sovereignty in monetary matters.

By this time the growth of the Euro-dollar market was some compensation for the decline of sterling. Bolton had been one of the first bankers to seize on this new medium as a way of operating internationally outside the reach of national exchange restrictions. In 1966 he explained the development of this new "international money market" in great detail to a conference organised by the Federal Trust for Education and Research. He firmly believed that this market had come to stay, and he heartily approved of its tendency "gradually to eliminate political frontiers in respect of international banking operations".

Although the Euro-dollar market has since grown much further both in volume and in technical diversity, this 1966 description of it is still one of the best available.

International Money Markets—1958-66:

In the past ten years the pattern of international financial transactions has been transformed by the emergence in the late 1950's of what has come to be known as the Euro-dollar market. This in turn has induced an unparalleled degree of co-operation and co-ordination between major financial centres through which a substantial portion of the world's surplus cash and capital resources is mobilised and channelled into the financing of international trade, and into the expansion and development of industry throughout the world. The flow of funds into this international money market has become large enough to influence domestic and foreign monetary policy in several countries and gradually to eliminate political frontiers in respect of the complicated nexus of banking operations flowing through foreign exchange and linked currency deposit transactions.

In view of the importance of the new market, we should examine its origins and the course of its development, while at the same time touching on some of the problems that have arisen. As a result of the imposition by the British authorities in 1957 of restrictions on certain types.of foreign trade financing, together with a bank rate of 7 per cent and a credit squeeze, transactions in Euro-dollars in London and in Switzerland began to assume significant proportions. The liberalisation in 1958 of exchange controls by a large number of monetary authorities resulted in the acceptance by the British and Swiss commercial banks of foreign currency deposits at more favourable rates of interest than were obtainable in New York. This was followed by progressive measures taken by the American administration to limit access by foreigners to the New York market. In the early days, the main activity between banks was in comparatively short term fixed deposits, but with experience it became possible to arrange overnight money and callable deposits; the market now provides medium term facilities to industry, term deposits and is moving into the short end of the capital market.

For a long time, there was thought to be some special mystique surrounding the Euro-dollar, and a certain amount of confusion has arisen as to what is meant by this term. Euro-dollars are merely dollars whose ownership temporarily changes hands at rates of interest above those permitted in the U.S.A. They have no separate rate of exchange and when we talk of Euro-currency rates, we refer to the rates of interest at which deposits are lent and borrowed. Both lender and borrower are frequently domiciled outside the U.S.A., but American corporations of all kinds, and the foreign branches of American banks, use the market extensively. In all cases when a Euro-dollar deposit is made or repaid a transfer of funds takes place either in or between banks in the U.S.A.

From very modest origins, the market, which is an integral part of the foreign exchange market, has developed into a highly technical process of spot exchange transactions, forward operations and deposits or loans; rates of interest vary not only for all the different currencies involved and the term of deposits, but also from hour to hour according to the pressures of supply and demand, the movements following the interplay of forward rates of exchange and many other influences. There are about seventeen different currencies involved, and you can imagine the possible permutations in the pattern of rates of exchange and rates of interest. This is one of the reasons why it was essential to have a main currency of reference, supported by a comprehensive and flexible banking system. Like the ocean, these markets are never at rest and, like women, never entirely predictable.

Many of the leading banks of the world now actively participate in the deposit and re-deposit of currency with each other, in the adjustment of their liquidity positions, entirely without security, and at rates of interest which are affected but not determined by the margins of the official money rates prevalent in the New York and London markets. This has been accomplished as a result of international needs, the enterprise of the banks, the confidence they have in each other and because the orthodox money markets have become too much subject to domestic requirements and political direction. The banks engaged in these transactions maintain a high degree of liquidity because they cannot have recourse to a central bank for assistance in case of any stringency occurring. The main if indirect support to the market is the modern phenomenon of growing and comprehensive central bank co-operation.

The international money market has attracted comment and criticism, partly as a result of the fact that, traditionally, any banking operation not conforming to a set of precepts laid down by established authority and hallowed by custom raises questions. Because international money market operations do not conform to precedent and are not subject to direct control, the suspicion arises that unsound practices will develop and the resources available will be used unwisely. I fail to see why anyone should think that regulation by exchange control, taxation or even central banking authority makes a serious banker more cautious in his handling of other people's money. There have indeed been several crises during the past few years on which the market's critics will seize to illustrate their point. There was the Japanese crisis of 1963 which was overcome largely by the action of the Bank of Japan with the support of the international banks. This was followed by the Italian stock exchange collapse which severely shook international confidence and set off a flight of capital from Italy. The assistance given to Italy by foreign central banks as well as her Euro-dollar borrowings during this period exceeded $750 million, and these funds were employed to increase domestic liquidity and to finance external transactions in order to reduce the claim on official reserves.

Then again, there was the Salad Oil affair in New York, and a number of other bankruptcies, the most recent being the Intra Bank of Beirut, which could have endangered the market if it had been basically unsound. However, the greatest test began in the autumn of 1964 with the sterling crisis which started with a massive outflow of funds from London and brought about pressures on international interest rates which have been rising ever since, partly as a direct result of monetary techniques and largely, so far as Britain is concerned, because of a loss of confidence. Close on its heels came a growing shortage of cash in the U.S.A., reaching a peak in August 1966 when American banking was on the verge of seizing up. Startlingly high interest rates were paid by the European branches of American banks, who drew $2 to $3 billion out of Europe, and, although the situation is now less tense, it would be imprudent to suggest that the troubles are over.

It is interesting to note that the State banks of many of the Iron Curtain countries operate extensively in the market with the Moscow Narodny Bank and the Banque Commerciale pour l'Europe du Nord firmly established in London and Paris respectively. To begin with, Eastern Europe appeared in the market primarily as lenders and were prepared to accept rates of interest fractionally lower than the prevailing norm in order to gain the confidence of the European banks. However, once they had established their connections they turned borrower, and the banks with whom they had frequently left deposits eventually developed a two way traffic. These contacts may have contributed towards easing the tensions between East and West.

Many are convinced that the market is a temporary phenomenon which will disappear, or at least cease to play the major role it presently does in the international credit system, once the peculiar and largely accidental set of circumstances which brought it into existence have ceased to operate. When Euro-dollar activities first developed, it was thought that the limits which practically every bank established on every other bank for forward exchange contracts would ultimately restrict the market. It was also felt that making deposits for periods varying from one day up to one year between banks would have some natural limitation and the market would reach saturation in a relatively short time. This, however, did not occur for a variety of reasons, for example many of the market's principal components are institutions whose credit rating cannot be measured by either traditional or practical standards, as for example, the central banks and the powerful international banks.

Many of the arguments put forward by the market's critics are based on the movement of interest rates in the U.S.A. At present, American banks are statutorily limited in the amount of interest that they can pay on certificates of deposit or time deposits. Even if the regulations were repealed or relaxed by the authorities, it is unlikely that there would be any marked effect on the Euro-dollar market, which would merely bid higher for its deposits in the knowledge that the ultimate borrowers are prepared to pay more for their loans. Historically, the United States does not favour a dear money policy, and the government even now is concerned at the level to which interest rates have risen lest they aggravate the inflationary pressures to which the American economy is already subject. At the time the President's guidelines policy was introduced in 1965, it was widely feared that the repatriation of funds to America would bring about a sharp contraction in the market. However, as a result of the pressure of constant demand on the supply of available dollars, interest rates hardened appreciably, thereby attracting a substantial flow of foreign-owned dollars. At the same time, the Italian commercial banks, acting under instructions from the Bank of Italy, whose reserves had largely recovered as a result of a heavy surplus in the balance of payments, began to reduce their external liabilities, thereby freeing a large amount of funds which reverted to the Euro-dollar market.

But quite apart from the question of interest rate differentials, there are some convincing reasons for suggesting that the market is here to stay. Whatever the outcome of discussions on international liquidity or the gold price, a new money market has been created which is more efficient in terms of the speed and the sophistication of its transactions than the older markets. It has shown its strength by withstanding, without apparent ill effect, a series of crises. By tapping previously unused liquid reserves of various sorts and origins, the market has made a contribution to the financing of international trade as well as to the financing of domestic operations.

I have dwelt at some length on the beginnings and expansion of the international money market because it provides the essential background to the rise of the international bond market. The failure of London since 1946 to restore its position as a market for sterling bond issues and the growing incapacity of the New York market to find capital for non-residents on any scale have brought about the gradual process of internationalising the provision of long term capital. Ten years ago, the first steps were timid as the sponsors were moving into completely unknown territory. These original transactions were difficult as, in the absence of a secondary market, placing with institutional investors provided the only method of distribution. But gradually syndicates of banks were formed to underwrite issues and this gave confidence to the investment houses in London, New York and European centres to negotiate loans and discuss terms in advance of issue. A further essential development was the deliberate organisation of a secondary market and a number of houses in Zurich, Geneva, Frankfurt, Brussels, Paris and London are now active dealers in most of the bonds already in issue and are ready to join in "selling groups" and make a market in new issues.

When the Vietnam war subsides, the inherent strength of the dollar and the U.S. economy will become self evident. The existing restrictions will be dismantled, interest rates will fall, and the New York capital market will be re-opened to foreign borrowers; but I believe that, unless the world collapses into a deep recession, the growing shortage of savings relative to capital requirements will become a major factor. In consequence, long term rates of interest will be established at relatively high historical levels. London will probably be unable to restore the international position of sterling except that when the exchange becomes more stable sterling area borrowing will become possible. But technical advances in industry are now so rapid and represent such a growing charge on limited capital resources that this, together with the greatly increased needs of the developing countries, will prevent the London and New York markets—even assuming the best—from being capable of meeting total demands. The future of the International Money Market is, I believe, assured and British industry should have access to it, particularly companies with a substantial foreign exchange revenue.

Despite the dangerous meddling and interference of governments in the workings of a highly sophisticated mechanism which they do not understand, and which they may seek to curb to satisfy their lip service to outdated dogma, the ceaseless ingenuity of the financial world will continue to provide essential facilities even in the most unfavourable circumstances.

Two years later the theme of the International Money and Capital Market as a new, lasting foundation of expanding world trade was further developed in the Ernest Sykes Memorial Lecture, delivered at the London Institute of Bankers in February 1968. Bolton now felt not merely sure that this market was sound but enthusiastic about its potential role: he described it as "the only practical basis upon which a future international monetary system can be built".

While economic theorists, central bankers and civil servants are pursuing tenuous schemes to secure an increase in the level of world liquidity commensurate with the spiralling development of the second industrial revolution, practical bankers in all countries have created a new market adapted to meet modern needs since the gold exchange standard was re-established at Bretton Woods in 1944. By building an apparatus in an amazingly short time for the collection and redistribution of the world's surplus cash and capital resources, the commercial banks have produced a unique machinery for serving the financial needs of the whole world, both East and West. "Professional" inter-bank and arbitrage operations, the technical basis of the International Money Markets, have made available short and medium term international working capital which would otherwise have been locked up in the restricted money markets of many countries where resources, if not immediately wanted for domestic needs, would remain sterilised. The recent growth of these markets has—significantly—followed the virtual closure of the world's two major capital centres, New York and London, to foreign borrowers.

During the last ten years, many variations on the original theme of interbank operations in short term deposits have been cautiously expanding and, in consequence, a market of such flexibility has been created as to begin to replace the financial services available in the pre-restriction heyday of London, New York, Paris, Berlin and Vienna. By establishing methods of mobilising what were formerly sterilised banking and capital resources and at the same time accelerating the velocity of circulation of these funds around the market, commercial bankers have succeeded—for the time being—in averting a major breakdown in the provision of finance for international settlements. Most leading banks in the world now deal actively in deposits with one another, adjusting their own liquidity positions, entirely without formal security, at rates which, while affected by world events in the same way as their purely domestic counterparts, are not subject to controls and restrictions imposed by nationalistic requirements, political, economic, social or otherwise.

Some criticism arises from this freedom, largely from the inherited beliefs we call orthodox banking derived from the completely different conditions and techniques that developed from the commercial banking practices organised under the gold standard. The commercial banks have achieved methods of dealing with only such self-imposed control, e.g., credit worthiness, as they wish to exert on one another, and the normal limitations of dealing particularly in forward exchange. National authorities, having learned that it is reasonable, politic, and within their powers to assume the management of their own economies, find the freedom of the Euro-currency market untidy because they are faced with the dilemma of choosing between allowing a substantial degree of freedom and total control of activities that should by definition be subject only to some form of international control.

There are those who consider that the market depends for its existence on a continuing deficit in the United States balance of payments and that, when the Vietnam war is finally settled and the huge overseas expenditure to support it is no longer required, the market will decline. Even were the Americans to cure their deficit entirely, this could only be achieved at the expense of other nations' surpluses, and this obvious fact seems to me to be the major contradiction of the argument that the International Money Market will disappear pro rata with the diminution of the U.S. deficit. In other words, either the American administration will fail to reduce the deficit even when the war ends or, if they succeed, then other economies—most probably developed economies—will go into much reduced surplus and even deficit on their own balance of payments. Either way, adequate liquidity will continue to exist for the market to be well serviced, even though it will be dealing more in currencies other than dollars. In any case, yen, francs, Deutsch-marks, etc., are perfectly acceptable to the market machinery as it is, and it would need little or no adjustment to cater for such a change of emphasis.

Some critics claim that the market is little more than a house of cards on a shaky foundation of untested credit and doomed to autodestruction with the first breeze of adversity. These critics fail to realise that the market is essentially the only practical method, however imperfect, to fill the vacuum which has developed in international finance since the last world war. Considerable evidence of the existence of such a vacuum was to be found, for example, during the 1950's when the dollar shortage, now called the shortage of liquidity, had a profound and restrictive effect on the development of the European and other industrialised western economies. Since those difficult days, the development of these economies has been greatly assisted by the American balance of payments deficit, albeit a dangerous method of providing an increased international liquidity. It is also important to maintain a sense of proportion about the size of the U.S. deficit which at, say, U.S.$4 billion per annum could be cured, given the political will, by a comparatively small transfer of resources in relation to the American GNP of $800 billion.

Continental Europe, with France in the lead, has been the most open critic of the British and United States policies of budget deficits. The follow-up of last November's run on sterling by an attack, however unsuccessful, on the dollar is an example of how the market provides what is the only possible framework to prevent a world-wide recession and all that such a dislocation of human existence would mean. If the French were to argue that current trends are leading to a world expenditure greater than world output, given limited world resources, and that the ensuing inflation will be insupportable, one could possibly find some common ground of agreement. As it is, they have clung to what Keynes called the "savage system", whereby our capacity to trade with one another is directly proportionate to the quantity of gold bearing dirt we scratch from the earth, less that amount of the metal worn on our persons or used in industry.

One can understand of course that the continental experience of badly managed paper currencies is such as to have developed into a positive phobia against relying on any monetary system divorced from gold. But the truth of the matter is that the U.S.A. is financing the growth of industry and trade throughout the world by its own deficit. Although the short sighted can argue that the United States are therefore getting more than their fair economic share of worldly rewards, even the most dogmatic among them cannot fail to observe that the major contribution to the huge improvements in the western world's standard of living is directly attributable to American oversea investment, and thus to its operating deficit. Whatever its current problems at home and abroad, the U.S. economy remains by far the strongest in the world. Whatever its short term difficulties, the U.S. dollar remains the world's strongest currency and, given time, the returns on U.S. investments will have an immense effect on the future "hardness" of that currency.

When the Vietnam war ends, it is reasonable to expect a reduction in the American balance of payments deficit, a strengthening of the U.S. dollar relative to other currencies and an immense increase in the activity of the International Currency Market. The European bond market will probably lose some business to a revived New York foreign bond market. But the pull of the European market will remain based upon the strength and expertise and techniques of the banking and financial structure that has been built up, and which is rapidly developing into a wider and more sophisticated capital market.

To return to the external claims, however, one must remember that markets in claims between one area and another are not a mystery. London's strength as a world financial centre is based to a large extent on the experience gained over several centuries in dealing with such claims. The only difference is that originally those claims grew with the Empire and world trade but, because of the enormous developments in world trade since the end of the last world war and the decline of the British empire and its currency, a growing volume of "modern" claims are now in currencies other than sterling. The underlying business and market techniques, however, remain unaltered.

When the leading monetary experts met at Bretton Woods in August 1944 to try to correct the faults of the pre-war years, and create a better system for the new world, there were those who, even then, foresaw many of the problems of the next twenty-five years; they recognised the need for a complete reappraisal not only of the traditional system but also of the complex thinking behind it. Unfortunately, instead of being allowed to design and construct a new system of international settlements capable of the expansion necessary to absorb increasing demands upon it, the pressures of traditional thought merely redrafted the old values and produced a structure which, with the advantage of hindsight, can be considered only as a temporary measure however great an advance in economic practice it then represented.

In the absence of a "world" central bank with the power to control the international market in a world currency, the International Currency Market represents not a second best alternative but the only practical basis upon which a future international monetary system can be built.

In spite of the physical distances between its participants, modern means of communication covering the whole world, together with the strength of the commercial banks, allow the development of a completely open market and the resulting competition maintains its continuing dynamism. The market is now so wide, both in its sphere of influence and range of services, as to be beyond the control of any one country—although of course it is quickly affected by events of world importance. The great contribution which the market has provided to improve international liquidity is irreplaceable. We should not forget in this context the growing co-operation between central banks for the purpose of maintaining as much order as possible in the exchanges. The major disturbance caused by the sterling crisis will inaugurate a stormy period of convulsive change and continuous anxiety. Central bank co-operation will be intensified and probably more attention will be given to the interest rate structure of the International Money Market as its important role in world finance will become greatly emphasised.

Unhappily, the reactionary monetary element on the continent is very much on top at the moment. In spite of this, the past decade has produced a financial organisation capable of taking advantage of the situation. We are working towards a truly international system; and the development of markets in Euro-currencies for short and medium term use has made people aware of the urgent need for the consolidation of the market and a greater understanding of its immediate and long term importance. All of us are familiar with the arguments about the attraction of gold as the sole basis of international liquidity. In this context we must take geology into account: there have been no gold discoveries of magnitude since the nineteenth century. Even if the price of gold were doubled or trebled, little increase in gold production (in terms of weight) would be seen. Gold is now in growing use in the arts and industry, and in the years to come gold will find itself in the same position as silver, where industrial demand is such that it is quite impossible to use silver as a monetary metal. Monetary authorities are, as you know, already engaged in devising new methods to ensure international liquidity. Progress will be slow, as the innate conservatism of the banking profession, combined with an understandable distrust of governments, rejects change; but in the interregnum, the International Money Market will become more and more important and play a greater role in the normal processes of foreign trade and finance.

Meanwhile the international position of sterling was rapidly becoming critical again. In 1967 a series of crucial strikes, followed by the closing of the Suez Canal after the Arab-Israeli war, once again deferred hope of getting British payments into balance. In any case inflation had continued despite the attempted retrenchment of 1966, and the idea that the problem was now insoluble without a devaluation of the pound was steadily gaining ground. British economists had held this view increasingly since 1961; by 1964 many of the Government's own advisers urged devaluation; in 1967 even central bankers abroad, and the staff of the International Monetary Fund and Bank for International Settlements, had lost hope that British payments could be restored to balance at the existing exchange rate. At each successive spasm of pressure on sterling it became more difficult to raise yet another hurried short-term credit; one European central bank governor, a good friend of Britain, said sadly: "The era of the telephone is nearly at an end".

Bolton, always a fighter, refused to accept defeat. In September 1967, when professional opinion was moving rapidly towards recommending devaluation as a deliberate policy, he set out his strong objections to this view in the bank's quarterly review. As usual he made little of the immediate relief to be gained, and let his mind sweep across the centuries.

The theory that a currency can be relieved of adverse pressures by devaluation is valid only in the very short run and only in respect of some of the pressures. Any country's balance of payments may be weak for reasons other than that its currency is overvalued, and there is no certainty that a devaluation will achieve more than a temporary reversal of an outflow of short term capital. In the simplest terms, funds that are taken out of a banking system because a devaluation is expected will flow back when it is no longer expected. There are two ways of eliminating the expectation: one is to devalue and allow the inflow of returning funds to create the impression that all problems have been solved; the other is to correct the basic imbalances that have given rise to the expectation. A devaluation that ignores and conceals basic weaknesses will be almost certainly followed by another.

Monetary history is substantially a record of steadily declining purchasing power interrupted by periods of apparent stability, the most recent being the seventy-five years before the 1914–18 War. Modern experience can be said to begin with Diocletian's decision in 301 A.D. (similar to the British Prices and Incomes Board) to prevent any further rise in the cost of living by the detailed exercise of central authority over all prices and wages. It is of interest to quote from Diocletian's Edictum de Pretiis, dictating maximum legal prices or wages for all important articles or services in the Empire. Its preamble attacks monopolists who, in an "economy of scarcity", had kept goods from the market to raise prices:

"Who is so devoid of human feeling as not to see that immoderate prices are widespread in the markets of our cities, and that the passion for gain is lessened neither by plentiful supplies nor by fruitful years, so that . . . evil men reckon it their loss if abundance comes. There are men whose aim it is to restrain general prosperity . . . to seek usurious and ruinous returns . . . Avarice rages throughout the world . . . Wherever our armies are compelled to go for the common safety, profiteers extort prices not merely four or eight times the normal, but beyond any words to describe. Sometimes the soldier must exhaust his salary and his bonus in one purchase so that the contributions of the whole world to support the armies fall to the abominable profits of thieves."

The emphasis was obviously on military expenditure, and this was not curtailed. In consequence, the success of the Edict was short-lived, and the experiment contributed to the total economic and political ossification of the Western Roman Empire, and thus to its decline and fall in the following century. Wars, pestilence, brigandage and the intermittent exercise of authority, destroying law and order, all contributed during the ensuing 1,500 years of Western Europe's history to reinforce man's distrust of investment in enterprise in favour of precious metals and stones and, where order prevailed, land.

The acceptance of the Pax Britannica during the nineteenth century provided the essential framework for the development of paper money and a deposit banking system. The five-pound note then circulated beside the sovereign and was regarded as good as gold and twice as convenient, and the bill on London provided international means of payment. The calamitous twentieth century, ushered in by peripheral conflicts, has seen the wholesale destruction of communities, the death by violence of many millions and the release of the forces of destruction inherent in all human beings. The "gold standard" began to collapse in 1917, and finally passed away between 1931 and 1933 leaving paper money and bank credit as the universal and only means of domestic and international payment. It has long been fashionable to give the gold standard most of the blame for the "stop-go" cycles of the last century and the early part of the twentieth century, which have usually been the result of domestic policies incompatible with membership of any international monetary system. Perhaps we have seen enough by now to have learned that getting rid of the gold standard does not get rid of exchange crises, booms and recessions.

Instead there has been added to them, with the help of "managed currency", a drift towards total instability in the value of money. Of course in theory a managed currency can be managed so that it only gives room for manoeuvre in economic policy in ways that are to everyone's advantage; but it does not work out like that. In effect, the money system is abused so as to give more rein to inefficiency in production and to overgrasping demands for money to spend—for governments and for personal incomes. It is an old tag that "inflation is the most inequitable form of taxation". But, with the money swindle, that is the way in which over-reaching demands from people and governments are paid for, and the way inefficiency is subsidised and perpetuated. It provides a soft option in the short run, of course; the practical problem is to get people to realise how short that run can become.

All governments at one time or another abuse the money system, and especially paper money, not realising that the stability and purchasing power of paper money does not rely on government fiat but fundamentally on the belief of a people in the survival of their country, in its stability and, above all, on their conviction that their institutions, including the legislature, are efficient and incorruptible. This is what is called "confidence" and where the beliefs are lacking no technical devices, even the most savage form of exchange control, will ensure the eventual survival of the currency. Since the 1914–18 war, we have had sufficient examples of the consequences of the abuse of paper money systems; yet much of current controversy still revolves around the economic effects of depreciating purchasing power—if anything with an emphasis on the benefits of depreciation. As usual, the historical consequences are treated with magnificent disdain because they have been universally political and therefore not easily identifiable by a world suffering from too much economic theory and statistical analysis. Examples are available in the state of China after the withdrawal, under American pressure, of silver from circulation in 1936; Germany and Italy in the 1920s and 1930s following uncontrolled inflation; and the situation of France in 1939–40 after twenty years of unstable government associated with a persistent depreciation of the franc. More recently, in Latin America, a simple lesson is being learned that weak democracies promote, but do not survive, persistent inflation. It would be most imprudent of British and American political parties to assume that "it cannot happen here".

The most disquieting aspect of the demand for a devaluation is that it would almost certainly come to accentuate the distortions that it was intended to correct. Experience in countries that have used devaluation as a corrective suggests that, once it has been used, it may too easily be used again unless the basic causes of inflation are attacked at the same time. Examples may be seen in Latin America of countries that have used devaluation as a regular instrument of policy; these might be studied by those who advocate devaluation for Britain.

Today's governments face the need to redress longstanding imbalances before inflation can be brought under control and the need for periodic devaluations eliminated. This indeed is the main lesson we should learn in this country from the experience of Latin America. The best that devaluation can do, if it is anything more than the inevitable acknowledgement of having allowed costs to get out of international line or of having the misfortune to rely for export earnings on a commodity that has become a glut on the market, is to give a little time to remedy basic weaknesses. If, however, there is a lack of will to deal with these weaknesses before devaluation, there is no reason to suppose that devaluation will create that will. If the basic remedies are lacking, devaluation becomes a habit.

Besides this, once devaluation becomes a frequently used instrument of economic management, the business community learns to take devaluation into all its calculations; exporters learn to withhold their exchange earnings from the market, importers stockpile goods in expectation of selling at higher prices, and exchange operators and speculators add to the pressure thus often precipitating the devaluation before it is really necessary. Situations of this kind have the further disadvantage of adversely affecting the confidence of foreign investors, who delay transfers of capital when a devaluation seems likely—which could mean that the investment is virtually never made—or, if they already have a stake in the country, remit their profits with extreme haste and in addition allow their business to become decapitalised.

The general argument derived from experience in Latin America and elsewhere—that devaluation may perpetuate weakness rather than reform it—is strengthened for Britain today by three considerations. First, that the immediate weakness of Britain's balance of payments may be very largely attributed to the country's foreign expenditure on official account. No doubt it is impossible wholly to disentangle the ramifications and interactions of private and official expenditure, but there is every appearance from the figures officially published about Britain's external payments that the private sector is more than paying its way, taking current and capital accounts together, and that it is the burden of transactions undertaken on government account that has forced the final total so often into deficit. These transactions obviously would not be affected by devaluation but depend entirely upon the Government's own decisions.

Secondly, with exports there is no real indication that Britain's competitive weaknesses are the consequence of high prices. Profit margins may well not be as high as they might be, but for how long would a devaluation remedy this? It is in fact well known that considerations of delivery, specification, design and other matters related to industrial efficiency are in general more important than prices in explaining Britain's export performance—a performance that remains far from wholly bad. These factors clearly would remain unaffected by a devaluation. Similar remarks may be made about the level of imports of finished industrial products into Britain. These often reflect a failure on the part of some of our industries to produce consumer goods of modern design or capital equipment of efficiency comparable to those of foreign origin. In considerations of this kind, price is less relevant than quality, appearance, or efficiency of operation, as the case may be.

Finally, in the public sector, whose balance-of-payments deficit is so important, a rise in the sterling cost of debt payments and other official commitments would doubtless call for higher taxation from which there would be no social benefit. The level of the public sector's real expenditure at home has shown itself uncommonly resistant to any curtailment; this too must mean it is the private sector that will bear the whole loss of real income and wealth that a devaluation would entail. In short, many inflationary pressures would be engendered throughout the economy, and it is optimistic to suppose that administrative restraints would hold them in check indefinitely. It is doubtful whether our prices and incomes policy is so strongly based that it could withstand additional provocations. And, as experience has shown, monetary restrictions applied to cost inflation can bring about a recession without halting the rise in prices.

In conclusion, it is imperative to emphasise that the fate of other economies is intimately linked to the future of the London market and the use of sterling in trade and payments. This is one of the terrifying responsibilities of any British Government, and for the near future it is an inescapable one because British banking and international services are for the time being irreplaceable; sterling therefore cannot be treated by any responsible British Government as solely a British problem. The domestic consequences of persistent inflation in Britain will have a profound impact on our political structure; they could perhaps even wreck the democratic process and spread chaos over a much wider area.

> It was no use. In November 1967 sterling was overwhelmed by yet another wave of foreign selling, and there was no more foreign help to be had without a change of the parity and a pledge of new policies. In the end the Government delayed its decision until the markets broke in panic and the pound had to be devalued in a disorderly rout, with very heavy, unnecessary losses on forward purchases and guarantees at the old rate. The sight of indecision and incompetence added to the general impression of hopelessness. This time even the more long-term holders of sterling balances, who had remained remarkably loyal throughout, began to pull out. After devaluation the overseas sterling area countries, which had still kept the bulk of their reserves in sterling, withdrew funds at such a rate that the situation was only stabilised after yet another international stand-by credit had been raised and a dollar guarantee provided for a large part of the sterling balances.
>
> Bolton described the devaluation of the pound from \$2.80 to \$2.40 as an "unmitigated disaster" and added that "any disruption of a delicately balanced international system has unforeseen and ever widening repercussions that rapidly lead to a deterioration of confidence and the undermining of political organisations and governmental institutions". In his review of the year 1967, written early in 1968, Bolton makes some bitter comment on "the weaknesses in our political structure that have helped to bring us to our knees".

The ripples of the sterling crisis are now beginning to spread throughout the world; in the few months since 18th November 1967 we have had a panic rush into gold; an attempted deflationary policy in Britain; a new political and strategic vacuum created in the Indian Ocean and the Far East; and the imposition of restrictions in the United States that will have the effect of introducing some deflation into Western Europe.

The naivety of those who advocated devaluation and the abandonment of the sterling system is now beginning to be exposed, for it is being demonstrated practically daily that all that has been done is to magnify our problems and leave the country more isolated than ever before. There has been no real solution of our foreign trade policy dilemma; in addition, our world influence is gravely diminished and if the international payments system is now imperilled, many will lay the blame at our door. Some attention should be given to the problem of ensuring our essential imports, on which the export drive depends; we may also have to consider, if the international exchange system moves into crisis conditions, how to conduct foreign trade in currencies other than sterling. Even so there is little doubt that at this point every effort should be made to restore the sterling system to working order. Even if this is achieved we shall only have turned the full circle, with no visible advantage except that experience will have revealed the errors of the false prophets.

Britain, now completely freed of its embarrassing legacy from the past, has much to be hopeful about. The British empire is now a matter of history; the Commonwealth, which we can neither finance nor defend, is in a state of suspended evolution; and of our great inheritance there now remains to us only our international services, such as banking, insurance, shipping and marketing, and the English language, on which to rebuild our future. We must abandon the presumption, based on nineteenth century shibboleths that have little meaning for today's generations, that it is our role to lead the moral conscience of the world; we should rather concentrate on expanding trade and financial relations with those with whom we have a natural affinity and long term friendship.

In this protracted process of disintegration, sterling virtually ceased to be acceptable as a reserve currency and lost much of its standing as a trading and financial currency. The sterling area was still tenuously held together by close technical co-operation between its central banks, but the foundations had been badly shaken. During 1968 confidence at home and abroad continued to weaken not merely because of the loss of material strength, but probably more because of the long delay in governmental action to "make devaluation work". Instead of the promised relief, there was renewed pressure, and the prospect was clouded by talk of still heavier deflationary policies to come, and a frightening load of short term debt to repay.

Throughout 1968 the gloom persisted; but towards the end of that year one could detect the first promise that the disaster of 1967 had not, in fact, been "unmitigated". The lower exchange rate of the pound did, after an unexpectedly long delay, stimulate exports and restrain imports, as well as add heavily to the net overseas income from investments and from financial and commercial services. Moreover, a new man was at the Treasury—a man of ambition and intelligence. As 1968 dragged on, decisions were at last being forced through the sluggish and bewildered Cabinet. Under insistent pressure from the I.M.F. a firm control of the money supply was introduced. A huge increase in taxation coincided with the culmination of a ten-year effort of the civil service to devise rules for a real control of Government spending. In the 1969 budget Mr. Roy Jenkins was able to undertake that the Government as a whole, including local authorities and nationalised industries, would not only have no "borrowing requirement" in 1969–70 but would actually produce a surplus of revenue for the first time in many years. This pledge was made good.

Taken together with a modest success in slowing down wage increases, these policies did make an impact on the formidable powers of inflation. In the course of 1969 the balance of payments at last moved into the substantial surplus that had been vainly sought for years. There is room for debate how far this fortunate turn was simply the response to devaluation and how much was contributed by the highly conservative fiscal and monetary policies which the Labour Government had adopted. Certainly, towards the end of 1969, money was coming back into London at a steadily growing pace; first the "lead and lags" of the long sterling crisis were unwound, then international traders and bankers rebuilt working balances in sterling which had been kept uncomfortably low, and finally foreign cash and investment funds began to flow in, drawn by the old magic of the City and the superiority of its technical facilities over other financial centres, as much as by relatively high interest rates.

No doubt the recovery was helped by the loss of confidence in the French franc during 1968, and the advent of a Socialist Government in West Germany in 1969 which was followed by the revaluation of the D-mark and a flight of both foreign and German capital out of marks. Nor did it restore anything like the old position of sterling as an international currency. But to some extent, and for the time being, virtue had earned its reward. Bolton would not be comforted. In June 1969, giving his personal view of the prospect to the London "Sunday Telegraph", he was still expecting the monetary crisis to continue and the situation to get out of hand. But there is a glimpse of his private hope: when the inevitable break with the past comes "we shall be stripped of many illusions and many incompatible policies will have to be abandoned". Then, at last, "our spirits will revive".

One of the features of the persistent monetary crisis has been the search for capital and the degree to which corporate treasurers and finance directors have to accept unorthodox risks if their companies are to be able to finance normal expansion plans.

The demise of the U.K. domestic capital market, accompanied by a realisation that this country is not able to support sterling in its traditional role as a medium for the finance of international trade, is playing a part in the growing malaise. The City, however, is used to invention in the face of misfortune, and has adapted the international currency market to assume some of the duties formerly undertaken by sterling.

So long as this market was used for its original purpose—the raising of funds for use largely by Europeans—the rates, being dependent solely upon the laws of supply and demand, remained at reasonable levels.

The arrival in the market of the Americans attempting to finance U.S. industry, however, has resulted in today's abnormally high rates and general indigestion in the market. It is not unfair to suggest that the American banking system is unconsciously exporting Washington's deflationary policy to Europe. The rise in interest rates has brought us uncomfortably close to conditions previously thought of as restricted to Latin America and Indonesia; the shortage of capital, which shows no sign of easing, has had the inevitable result of separating the richer countries in need of capital from the poorer, with an unavoidable widening of the gap between the developed and undeveloped countries of the world.

The monetary authorities of the leading countries now face a cruel dilemma as they are conducting monetary policies designed to offset the consequences of prolonged governmental abuse of the monetary system, without being able to influence the representatives of the electors responsible for fiscal policies.

When the Bretton Woods agreement was successfully concluded, there was little doubt in the minds of many of the participants that the final agreement establishing the I.M.F. was an uneasy compromise between those still passionately attached to the gold standard and others who were convinced that a partial restoration of the gold standard would be a mistake and that the barely submerged conflict would eventually emerge.

Broadly speaking, the conflict is between the Anglo-Saxons who believe in credit expansion based on paper money, and the Europeans who are wedded to price stability and tying currencies to gold. This underlies some of our current problems.

In those post-war days, the rehabilitation of a world partially destroyed by war represented a financial effort which the resources of the Western banking world could not sustain if the credit base had to be controlled according to the nineteenth century rules of the game. In addition, every country wanted either to modernise its existing industrial equipment or to industrialise.

Without the tremendous economic burden that had been accepted by the United States from 1946 onwards, there would have been no possibility of a reconstruction of the capitalist system. The burden of war-time debts and post-war refinance weighing upon the U.K., together with the consequences of the introduction of the welfare state, has proved to be more than the sterling system can bear.

An important watershed in the British situation was reached in 1952/53 when the Government of the day decided that Britain could not accept the strains that would arise if a policy of complete freedom in trade and finance were adopted.

Instead of going for a truly free market economy like the Germans we had a rather curious combination of socialism and freedom. The two do not mix and thus we have had a series of "stop-go".

From that time onwards, the British economy has consistently lost direction and is now facing greater difficulties than ever before.

In all the arguments about inflation and monetary stability, there seems to be little understanding of the fact that what is broadly described as inflation is inevitable when capital development tends to outrun savings.

The nearly unbelievable expansion in world trade has been consistently accompanied by rising costs and rising prices and it is very difficult to see how this expansion could have occurred without "inflation" becoming built in to the system. But the attempt to use exclusively monetary weapons to help resolve the position is likely, if persisted in, to produce some very unpleasant consequences unless accompanied by complementary fiscal policies.

The credit squeezes that are now going on in a number of countries, including the United States, Canada, the United Kingdom and France, will bring about great distress among small and under-capitalised business, and will lead to a major reduction in investment decisions by the larger companies.

The dilemma that Britain faces is probably more acute than those of the others because of the magnitude of our short term debt expressed in foreign exchange; the Government has consequently little freedom of action—the usual fate of the incorrigible debtor.

It is difficult to avoid coming to the conclusion that the situation is getting out of hand and that all we can do is to wait patiently for events to take over and produce their own solutions. But it would be very wrong indeed to assume that when the inevitable break with the past occurs we shall all be faced with disaster.

Certainly we shall be stripped of many illusions and many incompatible policies will have to be abandoned. But we shall be at the end of the long drawn out series of crises which have brought about such a loss of confidence in our country and our institutions, and our spirits will revive in an atmosphere of hope and belief in the future.

In September 1969, just as the revaluation of the D-mark ushered in a period of relative calm in the exchange markets, Bolton used the twenty-fifth anniversary of the Bretton Woods agreement to look back and look forward once again. Speaking to the Canadian Chamber of Commerce in London, he flatly refused to accept the easing of international monetary tension as the beginning of better times. Peering into the future of "a former imperial power reduced to a very modest world role", he warned that it was a dangerous illusion to think "that we have in the past twenty-five years somehow discovered the secret of stability, automatic growth and prosperity".

Speaking as one of the few surviving members of the British delegation present at Bretton Woods and the succeeding conferences, I cannot help wondering now whether the whole exercise was not a waste of time. We seem to be back at the beginning. Many of those present at Bretton Woods have now passed away; some were driven from their countries, or disappeared into concentration camps; others have committed suicide; and altogether there are such a small number of survivors that I thought—in this twenty-fifth anniversary year of

Bretton Woods—a look to the past and a glance to the future might be of interest to you.

Towards the end of the war, many in my field were in a state of nervous agitation about the necessity to put the post-war world right and avoid the dreadful mistakes of the twenties and thirties. The Fund and Bank were to be the main instruments, and a whole series of other international organisations were to be created under the umbrella of the United Nations. The organisations were created, but the plans and ideals almost entirely collapsed under the weight of normal human frailty. Nevertheless, something was accomplished, and certainly the position of the Western World would have been very much more unpleasant if there had been no World Bank and no generous American taxpayer to pour surplus wealth into Europe, South America, Africa and so on. And sterling would probably have disappeared long ago but for the support given by the International Monetary Fund. But what was an even more important achievement was that an exchange system—more pompously called the "international payments system"—was recreated; a process of central bank co-operation was developed and in consequence the Western World has enjoyed a twenty-five year period of prosperity without parallel in living memory. The phrase "economic crisis" has often been used during the fifties and sixties in connection with the turn of events in one country or another. But these so-called crises (too often of British origin) have all been surmounted, and have generally ceased to be "news" in a relatively short time. In fact, they have only been crises for those—like many of you here today—whose work lies in the sphere of international trade and finance.

I believe that most bankers would agree that the possibilities of the Bretton Woods Final Act have been very nearly exhausted; and unfortunately the governments of the countries originally responsible for developing the reserve currency principle—namely, the U.K. with sterling and the U.S. with the dollar—have so abused the system that it is now in mortal danger. Exchange arrangements have worked well enough to deal with the periodic exchange problems of the smaller countries—and even to deal with such serious difficulties as those suffered by Italy in 1964. But major problems have now arisen of a kind not foreseen twenty-five years ago. Such problems as the continuous deficits of the reserve currency countries, controversy about the future role of gold, vast movements of hot money, and world inflation, have increasingly taxed the ingenuity of those operating the international monetary system.

As far as sterling is concerned, its reserve currency role has been frozen and its role as an international trading currency almost eliminated, while a large part of the resources available for stabilising the international monetary system have been pre-empted for sterling's defence. The result has been that Britain, far from relieving herself of wartime financial burdens, is now even more heavily indebted at short and medium term. Almost all our reserves are borrowed—not owned; and additional sources of credit must be very limited. This is the answer to anyone who expresses satisfaction at the advances in Britain's welfare and prosperity in the years since the war. How an increase, or even the maintenance, of prosperity, is to be reconciled with the repayment of our obligations has yet to be convincingly explained.

The problems created by the deficit in the U.S. balance of payments have been of a different order; and measures taken to eliminate the deficit may carry rather more dangerous implications than the continuation of the deficit itself. The commercial banks—operating internationally—may claim the credit for creating the Euro-currency market and so utilising the surplus dollars that might otherwise have been sterilised in the central banks of the surplus countries (or converted into gold), and in so doing have provided the world with a truly international capital market. But great strain has been placed on the international currency market by the demands made on it from the U.S.A. itself, as U.S. banks seek relief from their liquidity problems by bidding for dollar deposits in the market at unprecedentedly high rates. In the twenties and thirties we used to complain that all governments in some measure of domestic distress were engaged in "exporting unemployment". It is perfectly fair today to complain that the U.S. Government is deliberately "exporting deflation"—deflating the world economy by encouraging the American banks to bid for foreign owned dollar deposits at any price thus raising interest rates to ridiculous levels—even in countries enjoying large balance of payments surpluses.

This week the International Monetary Fund and World Bank assemble in Washington for the annual meetings. Since the last meeting, the world has seen upheavals in the foreign exchange markets, an election in the United States with consequent changes of policy in

South East Asia, and a parity readjustment of one of the world's major currencies. The only event that has been expected and has not materialised has been an open declaration of war in the Middle East. While no actual breakdown has occurred, an almost permanent state of unsettlement continues in the currency markets of the world. Central bank co-operation has staved off the worst excesses of speculative fever seen at the time of the sterling devaluation in 1967; but the handling of the French franc devaluation has delivered a body blow to mutual co-operation in central banking circles.

We cannot avoid the very real possibility of a complete breakdown of the international payments system as each individual nation blindly adopts self-regarding policies and fails to agree on universal plans to restore confidence in paper money. The tidal waves of money movements represent not so much speculation as national and international distrust of money. The present I.M.F. meeting will almost certainly fail to produce any new and original ideas and the proposals generated at the meeting will inevitably clash with the interests of individual participants, with protagonists of a return to the gold standard, and with the natural conflict between creditors and debtors. A compromise, introducing SDRs, will emerge; and this belated proposal provides some hope for the future. But in terms of world needs the mountain has laboured mightily to bring forth a mouse.

The extreme financial indiscipline and almost uncontrolled inflation that has affected a minority of Latin American states is, we hope, unlikely to be repeated in the industrialised countries. But Latin American experience is instructive. Some of its more important aspects are:- the primary, if not exclusive, role of excessive government expenditure perpetuated by overstaffed bureaucracies and inefficient state-run enterprises; the destruction of such capital markets as existed and the collapse of savings; the inculcation of "inflation-mindedness" among all classes and the diversion of much energy and ingenuity into staying in the perpetual race to keep income ahead of the daily price rise; the folly of governmental attempts to maintain an artificial structure of interest rates; the persistence of price rises even in periods of economic stagnation; and above all the tremendous efforts and sacrifices necessary for ultimate stabilisation. Parallels are beginning to be found in North America and Europe as excessive government expenditure has been allowed in many countries to proceed too long unchecked. Inflation is so well established that capital markets are ceasing to function. The Latin American political lesson is that persistent inflation destroys democratic organisation and that financial law and order can then only be restored by dictatorial methods of government.

It is easy to criticise people in positions of responsibility including politicians, central bankers and so on, for failing to take action to prevent what all of us fear most, namely capital starvation and the breakdown of capital markets. As an old central banker myself, I feel strongly that the use of nineteenth century monetary weapons to solve the completely different problems of the twentieth and twenty-first centuries will end in the creation of worse problems. Monetary authorities are too often engaged in papering over the cracks and trying to persuade the business and investing public that stability is either here or just around the corner. In my opinion, this attitude produces the worst possible results, especially if there is an inbuilt economic instability in the country brought about by political parties promising more than the economy can, or the individual is willing to produce.

If we are to anticipate the future of a former imperial power reduced to a very modest world role, I would suggest that H.M.G. consider plans based on a world suffering from a population explosion and the probability of shortages of food, energy and raw materials. The word "planning" is now a term of abuse, but I suggest H.M.G. should concentrate on ensuring the provision of these vital imports with say a fifteen-year plan combining ownership of foreign resources and inter-governmental agreements. Taxation laws that drive mining companies and others engaged in commodity production out of the United Kingdom should be changed in favour of attraction rather than repulsion. Every effort should also be made to encourage the exploitation of Britain's natural resources—as is being half-heartedly done in the North Sea.

Any form of gold standard should be progressively abandoned, if only for the reason that in a few years time the industrial demand for a shrinking gold output will leave little or none available for reserve requirements. The present two tier system foreshadows the return eventually to a completely free gold market, governments and central banks retiring from their present position and leaving the price to fluctuate according to supply and demand. Such a change in monetary policy would leave exchange markets as the dominant monetary influence, driving central banks and governments to combine to produce a system designed to maintain and expand world trade. The objective would be an international monetary authority to produce order where disorder and anxiety and distrust now reign.

I would also recommend that, as the U.S.A., Great Britain and Canada have decided to destroy their own markets in government securities, they should consider removing government securities (other than Treasury Bills) from the backing of the note issue. At the same time, particularly in the U.K., they should review the orthodox ratios of the commercial banks based on their holdings of government securities. In current and future monetary experience, with the near certainty of creeping inflation and consistently rising prices, it is not very far short of madness to regard short and medium term government securities (other than Treasury Bills) as offering any degree of liquidity. The time is coming near when respect for paper money, as it cannot be restored through gold, must be improved by other policies. The first is well known and well worn, viz., a reduction in government expenditure to a level consistent with an acceptable level of taxation, and related to the minimum volume of private savings consistent with the capital demands of industry. The second is to replace government securities as a backing to the note issue with the Government's holdings of marketable securities, gold, silver, uranium oxide, and comparable expensive metals, saleable real estate, commodities, valid claims on foreign governments, etc. It will appear a mixed bag, but public opinion is likely to be more reassured by it, than by the Bank of England's issue department showing over £3,000,000,000 of unmarketable government securities as sole backing to the note issue—and it may provide some check to the issue of paper money.

Any contention that we have in the past twenty-five years somehow discovered the secret of stability, automatic growth and prosperity is a dangerous illusion. The continuation of this prosperity depends more than ever on the ability of those in positions of responsibility and the situation is one that will require the utmost exercise of skill on the part of business management. Politicians and bureaucrats will eventually have to accept the fact that while they persist in using outmoded and irrelevant methods of monetary management no one is going to believe either in the money they issue, or in the infallibility of their economic judgements, or in them as leaders of the community.

THE WESTWARD POLICY CONFIRMED

As an opponent of British participation in the European Economic Community, Bolton was irritated beyond endurance by "Britain's second and foolish attempt to join the E.E.C." (in May 1967), and he took a leading part in organising a private feasibility study of an alternative concept: a North Atlantic Free Trade Association. This "would embrace Britain, the other members of EFTA, the United States, Canada and some of the other "old dominions" and perhaps Japan; the merit of this plan (he wrote in 1968) is that it would provide a realistic trade policy for Britain with solid commercial links with countries that are major producers of Britain's vital imports". He was impressed with the need to associate closely with the main sources of our imports of food, raw materials, and energy. As for the danger of domination by U.S. industries, he believed that the reduction of tariff barriers would make little difference to that trend.

In June 1968 he explained the scheme to a meeting of the London Chamber of Commerce.

The European Economic Community arose from the debris of post-war Western Europe, and in particular from the determination of a group of gifted Roman Catholic statesmen who decided to rebuild, in effect, a Rhineland Confederation with the addition of Italy. Out of this grew the Treaty of Rome in 1957, which the Six signed for many reasons including a declining faith in American leadership aggravated by what appeared to be the pro-Egyptian policy of the American administration and the consequence this would have on European communications with the East; these fears have of course now been realised and Europe's sea communications are now dependent upon the good will of South Africa and whoever controls the Panama Canal. Western Europe believed it needed a stronger union to enable it to decide its own policies in detachment from both the United States and Russia. De Gaulle and Adenauer organised the Community as a Franco-German dominated group and together they vetoed the entry of Britain which they regarded as an American satellite.

Over the last two decades, Britain has dismantled the empire and downgraded the Commonwealth. I refer particularly to Canada, South Africa, Australia and New Zealand. Looking back on my career in the banking world, I have seen this country decline in power and self-confidence, alternately taking responsibility for policies we have not the power to carry out and weakly evading responsibility for other matters—consistently following alien leadership and living under a blanket of compromise and mediocrity. If we, as a nation, are not to slip further into political oblivion, we need a new revelation and inspiration.

We should dismiss any further attempts to amalgamate ourselves with the European Economic Community, which is now little more than the Napoleonic conception of continental Europe under the leadership of a visionary who has failed in a hopeless attempt to recreate the past. There are many Europeans who dislike the present shape of the Community, but I believe that, even if they succeeded in making EEC more outward looking, Britain needs a wider vision. My objections to Britain attempting to join EEC have always been political. The history of Europe is strewn with object lessons suggesting that unification by a voluntary process is highly improbable. The two world wars started as European civil wars, and Europe was in the end defeated. Europe's imperial possessions were lost irretrievably, social structures were destroyed and in most cases the political roots of each country were poisoned.

The post-1945 recovery, largely the product of Russian/American hostility—although American generosity was of unparalleled magnitude—has now probably passed its peak. In spite of the splended efforts of the Brussels technicians in forging the structure of EEC common tariffs, the process of political unification has not been successful. While De Gaulle carries much of the blame for the revival of European nationalism, he cannot be blamed for the impending break-up of Belgium into three tiny parts, the consistent rise in the influence of the Italian Communist Party, the failure of the policy of unification of West and East Germany. If we were to become embroiled in all the current problems of Western Europe as a direct participant, we would have no time nor energy left to take care of our own affairs; and Europe would certainly remain totally uninterested in the problems of modernising British industry, the colour question, relations with the Commonwealth, and so on.

I believe therefore that for the future survival and prosperity of Britain, we must look to a trading and financial alliance primarily with America and Canada. The foundations were laid in the seventeenth century, when a small number of Britons established themselves in the New World; they were the beginning of links that over the years have grown between Europe and the West. In spite of the American civil war and the war of Independence, close economic ties were developed between Britain and America. American raw cotton fostered the growth of the Lancashire mills; North American wheat became the basis of the British loaf; and British manufactured goods were exported to the United States in spite of the emergence of formidable tariff barriers. British capital was invested in the American developing industries such as mining and railways. British educational philosophy had a marked effect on American schools and colleges.

I have written and spoken against the conception of the United Kingdom becoming a part of Western Europe politically, and just over a year ago I joined the Atlantic Trade Study, an independent non-party group formed to sponsor a programme of studies on the implications of Britain taking part in an open-ended Atlantic based free trade area. This group has received substantial support from many of our leading industrialists and bankers. The studies that the ATS have published or will publish explore the problems and background of NAFTA, a subject that this country should have at least some basis of research on which to fall back when the people finally realise that if we are to exist at all as a nation we must take immediate steps to widen our trading and free tariff areas.

The European Free Trade Association—consisting of Britain, Sweden, Norway, Denmark, Finland, Switzerland, Austria and Portugal—has proved a highly successful tariff free market. In just over six years, it has achieved complete industrial free trade while still permitting its members to follow whatever foreign policies they wish. Trade between its members has more than doubled, and it could be possible for Eastern European countries such as Yugoslavia and Poland to join whereas the Rome Treaty would make it impossible for them to join EEC.

Britain obtains well over 60 per cent of its imports from outside Western Europe, and about the same figure for exports go to those countries. The majority of our essential imports—dairy produce, meat, grain, sugar, tea, oil, timber, mineral ores, wool and cotton—come very largely from North America, Australia, New Zealand and countries in EFTA. It is therefore with these countries that an organised trading area is most logical. I should like to reiterate my reasons for believing firmly in NAFTA as the basis of a future trading policy for the people of Britain:—

1. We should be joining our natural trading partners in parts of the world which, to a large extent, are English speaking.
2. The growth of the population and production of the United States, Canada, Latin America and Australia will enable our country to expand a two-way trade. The natural resources of these areas will provide a substantial basis for industrial and economic growth. The gross national product of Canada has been estimated to grow by 5.2 per cent a year between 1965 and 1977; higher than that of any country in the EEC. The gross national product of the NAFTA countries (that is the United States, Canada and the EFTA countries) is expected to be $1,375,000 million by 1977, compared with $453,000 million for the EEC.
3. Britain would have control of its international trading policy with countries outside the NAFTA block. We would be able to expand freely our interests with the Communist bloc countries—a field in which we are already making progress and on the whole are welcomed.
4. Britain would maintain complete control over its internal laws—the Rome Treaty does not permit complete freedom of laws.
5. Food prices would rise only as world prices rise. The cost of most foods in EEC is considerably higher than in Britain because we import from the cheapest source whereas EEC agricultural prices are based on the highest cost producer.

6. It has been estimated that the loss to the United Kingdom balance of payments on joining EEC would be between £500 and £1,000 million per annum.*

Finally, we should never forget that Europe, exluding the Soviet Union, the last remaining imperial power, consists of a large number of medium and small countries with no stable political structure; with social tensions reflecting the clash between modernity and inherited social and religious traditions; and dependent for survival on material prosperity. The two wars destroyed much more than inherited wealth, empires and cultures; an atmosphere of irresponsibility and a cynical disbelief in religion, politics and morals prevails, and it may take generations before stability can be regarded as a normal experience. The recent French revolutionary situation may be regarded as an example of the basic instability of the European countries, an example that may be followed by Belgium, Western Germany and Spain.

We have not been occupied and we have sister communities in Canada, Australia, New Zealand as well as a more remote relationship with the U.S.A., none of which has suffered the traumatic experience of unsuccessful war and enemy occupation. It is this violent difference between domestic experience over two generations which makes a common monetary policy practically impossible. The ordinary public of these countries, Frenchmen, Germans, Belgians, Italians, have little conviction either in the survival of their governments or in the paper money issued by the respective monetary authorites. In consequence, the monetary authorities must attach their currencies to gold and constrict their economies to the irrational and rigid frame of the gold standard. This remains a total obstacle to Britain joining Western Europe, but on the other hand is a major incentive attracting us towards an expanding community such as the old members of the Commonwealth and the U.S.A.

* In February 1970 the British Government estimated the cost as between £100 million and £1,100 million a year, depending on the outcome of negotiations and other variables.

PROSPECTS AND POLICIES 1969-1970

In October 1969, when new negotiations for British membership of the European Common Market seemed to be approaching, Bolton gathered all his accumulated arguments against this policy into an all-out attack. In an article called "Britain's European Dilemma" which appeared in the London journal "Euromoney" he argued that the union of Western Europe could only be achieved, if at all, by a rigid framework of pooled sovereignty with a written constitution, which none of the nations concerned would ever accept. He predicted that political instability in Italy and France, and the German urge to re-unite, will produce explosive tensions which Britain as a member would be quite unable to influence. And if, as he suspects, America and the Soviet Union were to reach some kind of understanding on Europe, he would expect the "inherent tribal animosities of Europe" to erupt again.

These political objections always weighed more heavily with Bolton than the estimated economic balance, but in this field, too, he believed the disadvantages would be greater than the benefits. His passionate opposition to the whole idea of joining the E.E.C. began in the late fifties as a mere suspicion; how this attitude gradually developed into a rigid position can be traced throughout this book. But never before 1969 had he taken his stand with such fierce indignation, or raised his voice in such concentrated warnings, as in the paper which follows.

The leaders of our political parties are committed to the policy of Britain's membership of the EEC, irrespective of older economic and political relationships such as those that once inspired the Commonwealth; and the active protagonists of this policy are engaged in persuading the people of these islands that membership of the EEC is the only desirable fate for them and their children. The issues are so diverse that statistical justification can be found to support any view; This makes it difficult for sceptics to argue rationally with romantic enthusiasts. We live in an age of high pressure advertising, and the popular term "Good European" is a splendid example of a meaningless slogan invented to cast doubt upon any critic of Europeanism. "Good" in this context can mean bad in another and a "good" European may well be a bad man. I doubt, for example, whether the Aztec and Inca peoples regarded the Spanish as "good"; or whether the African tribes appreciated the "good" intentions of the many European countries involved in nineteenth century colonisation; the British invasion of the Orange Free State at the turn of the century, based on very dubious justification, reaped the usual harvest of death and disease as well as the undying hatred of the Boers; and civilised "Good Europeans" have been responsible, since the turn of the century, for the slaughter of tens of millions of their own kind in the two most barbarous and evil wars in the history of mankind. It is very doubtful whether we have changed our inherent characteristics; with the exception of Russia, we have simply become less powerful. The raison d'être of politics is power, and European unification could—in the long run—easily come to have more aggressive undertones than current propaganda likes to suggest.

The economic argument for Britain to join the Common Market is simple: our prosperity depends on our ability to sell abroad an increasingly sophisticated range of industrial products, and for this reason we have, since the war, supported movements towards tariff reduction and free trade. We now need unrestricted access to a larger market; because of its increasing size and complexity, the economy of an industrial nation such as this requires a wider scope than is afforded by our home market alone. Under Common Market arrangements, Britain would, of course, have to accept increased competition at home, and it is predictable that our modern and dynamic industries would gain from new export opportunities while the unregenerate would suffer from increased competition and would eventually face the choice between modernisation and disappearance. What is much less clear is the net effect on the balance of payments during the transition years when British industry endeavours to adapt itself—offensively and defensively—to the wider market.

Opportunities for increased industrial exports, particularly in the longer term, and perhaps faster economic growth through association with a more dynamic continent, no doubt offer the main advantages to be gained from entry to the EEC, but the main and quite inescapable economic disadvantage is that Britain must buy a large part of the nation's food requirements on less favourable terms in Europe instead of buying in the cheapest market; or, if we continue to buy our supplies from outside the EEC, we shall have to make a substantial contribution to the Common Agricultural Fund. The direct cost of food to the consumer will go up steeply enough, but the total exchange cost of the country's food purchase abroad, including payments to the EEC, could be even higher and this in itself must have some adverse effect on industrial costs and prices. For politicial reasons it is scarcely conceivable that continental Europe will ever agree to become an open market in food, or that the Six would not insist on Britain becoming a market for a substantial part of their surpluses.

The effect on the cost of living of a change in the British system of agricultural support from one of deficiency payments to one of higher market prices may be partly offset by a decrease in budgetary expenditure under this heading; but it would be foolish to expect, in view of the relentless rise in Government expenditure, that this would be followed by a reduction in taxation or that wage claims consequent on the increased cost of food would thereby be moderated.

The official view of the likely impact on the balance of payments is that "it is almost impossible to get accurate figures at the present time". But this aspect of Britain's entry into the EEC is crucial; Britain already has a formidable task to perform over the next five years or so, if we are to avoid default on our short term foreign debt. It is of the utmost importance that the Government should not join the EEC blindly, as an act of faith, but should take the British people into its confidence and be more precise about the additional burdens to be assumed.

So much for some of the economic problems that will arise from British membership of EEC. But, if we are to become part of Western Europe, what would seem to me to be of even greater importance, is that the British people should have a precise description of Western Europe as it has been and some assessment of what it may become.

The history of Europe over the past two thousand years bodes ill for ideals of "unity" which derive partly from the inheritance of the Christian Church, supported by an educated minority force-fed on Greek and Latin history and literature, and partly from the realisation that two exhausting wars have reduced the former Western European powers to a position of relative feebleness. The western Roman Empire collapsed in the fifth century, and for the next thousand years anarchy and violence reigned unchecked over many areas of Europe, but oral memory and the Catholic Church kept alive the memories of peace and law under Rome. Today it is often forgotten that law and order are sustained by and dependent upon the ultimate use of force, and that the relative peace and discipline of Rome was entirely the result of a superb military machine backing up strong government and a competent civil service. Our two most recent examples of European unification are represented by Napoleon and Hitler, both of whom ruled continental Europe from the Pyrenees to the Pripet Marshes while—and only while—they had supreme military power.

To me, the conclusion—in present conditions—is that a unified Europe can only succeed if it is solidly based on agreement on a common currency, a common language, a common legal system (Roman and Napoleonic law being in direct conflict with Anglo-Saxon common law) and, above all, a written constitution. Without a formal and binding framework, the whole campaign must begin to assume the appearance of son-et-lumière—the illusion disappearing as the grey shapes of old, turbulent, wicked Europe re-emerge.

It will certainly be difficult for the British, with our long experience of pragmatic political processes, to envisage any sort of written constitution. Nor can we be encouraged by the present political state of Europe. A collapse of parliamentary institutions in Italy cannot be excluded; and while parliamentary democracy may survive in France, despite a long history of administrative ineptitude, the reign of de Gaulle may yet be recalled with nostalgia if the return of party politics does not produce law and order—and the illusion of grandeur. An even greater source of political anxiety lies in the future of Germany, the major economic and financial power in the Community today: for Western Germany is only one half of Germany and the objective of re-unification remains at the core of Western policy, compounded in part of the need to resist potential Russian expansion, and in part of the belief that a divided Germany creates an instability in itself dangerous to peace. If, however, East and West Germany were re-united, the resultant combination would certainly dominate Western Europe—even if Britain had been incorporated.

Western Europe will, in any event, have to react to changes of foreign policy by other countries that have an impact on world affairs. For example, there is some evidence pointing to changes in Russian and American attitudes; under economic, social and other pressures, there appears to be a movement towards something in the nature of an understanding. Peace may break out—and the effects on Western Europe are likely to be dramatic. The widespread feeling of insecurity, which has been the main impetus behind NATO and "unification" as expressed by the Treaty of Rome, would in part be removed. The inherent fissiparous tendencies and tribal animosities of Europe, suppressed to a limited extent since 1945, will break through and Western Europe will be revealed as a group of small, relatively unimportant, countries whose previous world roles have been lost for ever during the thirty years conflict from 1914 to 1944. One can sympathise with British political party leaders who have an urgent—perhaps subconscious—desire to play a more important part in a larger European scene; but they overestimate their political skills, particularly in view of their U.K. performance, which would be lost in the witches' brew of political Europe from the 1970s onwards. They will have to make do with the present parochial problems of the United Kingdom, unless they are prepared to sink their personal ambitions and concentrate on a twenty-five year plan to include the following objectives:

1. The co-ordination of all forms of transport and energy, in terms of rationalisation and capital development on a Western European basis, designed to serve the European community economically and efficiently.
2. The examination of all forms of monetary organisation for the purpose eventually of introducing a credit and paper money system that will not be in a permanent state of emergent crisis. It is important to realise the width of the gap that exists between continental European and Anglo-American experience in money matters. In Western Europe, there is a natural suspicion of the

nature and future of paper money and of an expanding banking credit system—the outcome of a history of continuous military conflict resulting in a distrust of fiat money and a determination to rely upon personal protection against loss. The dollar/sterling system has developed in completely different circumstances, and any attempt to revive gold standard restrictive practices will be rejected by business, industry and finance in dollar/sterling countries.

3. The examination of potential combinations in selected industries, together with the concomitant trade union organisations, where it is evident that size is more important than quality. It seems possible, for example, that automobile production has now reached a point of time when creative development has ceased and, therefore, a variety of producers is self-defeating. There are probably other industries where unit cost of production is more important than any other factor.
4. The encouragement of travel and common cultural development and a movement—no matter how slow—towards a European language—which, given our national linguistic ineptitude, would probably have to be English. All this could bring some measure of successful unification, but if the emotional content in political organisation—viz., language, religion, sovereignty and party politics—is to be given priority, then failure is practically certain.

The youth of this country, feeling the need to lead their lives in an expansive society with room to move freely and, perhaps, make a fortune, emigrate to Australia, Canada, South Africa and the United States; there are no language problems, the legal systems are based on British experience and philosophy, social organisation and living standards have much in common. It is impossible to regard continental Europe as it now is as a place for the young to spread their wings and make a satisfactory living. The most likely consequence of our joining the Community would be a movement of Europeans on low living standards, e.g., Sicilians, into Britain to take advantage of our system of social welfare.

Britain gained real strength and stability only after the great and nearly empty continents of the New World and Australia were discovered. We are still growing with these expanding countries, and it seems probable that a national revival is possible only from a combination of the expansion of emigration, technology, trade and finance where we still have great potential for further growth and as a partner in the expansion of the developing world.

I find it impossible to avoid a conclusion that behind much of current political and economic philosophy is a fascination with size. This is to some extent the effect of American mass production technology which is slavishly being copied in other countries leading to the parrot-like repetition of the slogan "productivity", as the cure of all economic problems. Size brings in its wake other nearly insoluble problems, particularly in the fields of management and labour relations, and we have startling examples of these in our own arthritic monsters such as British Rail and the British Steel Corporation, where insubordination and cumulative losses seem inevitable. But when this philosophy is concentrated on power politics reflected in a policy of "unifying Europe", we are entitled to ask whether such a policy—if successful—would contribute towards stability and peace. I suggest that the odds are against such a combination helping to produce a peaceful world, and that better prospects for a peaceful world lie in the maintenance of the present linguistic and territorial divisions of Europe.

In an interview with the London magazine "The Banker" published in February 1970, Bolton expressed his views on the development of BOLSA and went on to refer to broader subjects: the decline of sterling, the prospects of gold, and the growing competition between British and American banks. This is one of the few occasions when he revealed when and why he decided that sterling was doomed as an international currency.

Sir George, BOLSA is now an international bank. What were the major steps taken over the past ten years in achieving this position?

The major steps taken to convert BOLSA from its role as a regional bank to an international bank included: a deliberate withdrawal from sterling activities in the belief that the international use of sterling would virtually cease; the organisation of an active exchange department; a decision that our responsibility lay in assisting the growth of the host countries more than the bank being regarded as a vehicle for the finance of British trade; and a decision to buy deposits at the going rate rather than solicit industrial companies to become customers, which led to our becoming an active factor in the international money market.

What prompted you to take such a pessimistic view of sterling?

Mainly the discussion, among economists and politicians, of the need to restrict sterling's international role, so that they would be much freer to deal with our affairs with only a domestic currency; and the consequences of this general economic controversy have moved in one direction only: the decline in the pound's use overseas. Moreover our decision has been justified in that the Bank of England now refuses to allow sterling to be used for transactions between third countries, and the London market for foreign borrowers has been closed for some time.

Do you regard London as a natural base for such international operations or could they be undertaken more easily from, say, New York or Zurich?

London is a natural base for international operations because of the high concentration of experience, expertise and intelligence in the City of London. In spite of the difficulties brought about by restrictions and exchange control, it is doubtful whether these advantages can be found in any other city. The factor that will determine the fate and future of international banking is political stability more than anything else.

Why do you think that the City of London has survived as a financial centre since the war, in spite of a succession of sterling crises?

The international service capacity of London has developed with the growth of the empire and with technical progress; our international services are now comprehensive. They have taken many generations to perfect and have earned the respect of the rest of the world. Another factor is the risk-taking habit of the average Briton who is prepared to take very great risks for the sake of capital gains.

Do you regard the decline in the use of the pound as a reserve currency as a threat to the City's operations or does it not matter what currency is used?

The collapse of the sterling system, partially deliberate, partially inevitable, is an unmitigated disaster. It has left the world with only one currency, namely the U.S. dollar, which in itself is suspect, as an international means of communication; and this may prove to be an inadequate substitute. The City can to a limited extent use any currency to finance operations, but I suspect that the biggest loser will be industry.

On the wider question of international monetary management, what do you regard as the major threats to world currency stability at present?

The greatest threat to currency is the growing distrust of paper money by all classes of people in most countries. This is partially the result of central banks becoming "the creatures of the Treasury", but the more important reason has been the continuing abuse by governments of the monetary system for the purpose of favouring the electorate.

How has this developed?

A central bank, even if it is independent, must take account of Government policies. If it is not independent then it is less able to stand up to Government pressure to provide finance for social and even political purposes. This has happened in practically every country: Britain, Canada, the U.S., France and so on. It has engendered a general distrust of paper money.

Do you see any future monetary role for gold?

The present monetary role of gold is clouded by emotional and subjective considerations that have little to do with basic realities. America, which plays the dominant part, is anti-South Africa largely because of the domestic problem of Black Power, and there is undoubtedly a feeling in strategic circles in Washington that inability to sell gold in large quantities may affect Soviet Russia's strategic designs. In the long run, it would appear that there is an inadequate supply of gold available in the ground to finance world trade at a time of a population explosion and an expansion of industrialisation in very many countries. If the general instability of the international payments system becomes more apparent, it is possible that an attempt may be made to bring back gold as representing a standard of value more acceptable than governmental promises. But in general, I feel that the paper money system that exists today is too deeply entrenched for any return to a metallic standard.

In the operations of your own bank you are meeting with competition from U.S. banks virtually everywhere. Does your connection with Mellon help in this respect?

Our association with the Mellon Bank in Pittsburgh has brought us into direct contact with the industrial giants of the United States. Most of these have operations of one kind or another in Latin America and we are therefore able to compete with American banks on ground floor terms. Apart from this situation, the fact that we are British and not American is of great assistance in many countries.

Do you face the threat from the establishment of so many American banks in London and elsewhere with equanimity?

I do not think of this in terms of threats to the efficiency of theBritish, French or German banking systems. The Americans are adding to their banking capacity overseas, because of the needs of their large American customers. In the London banking community they find that competition is of a very different nature from that of their own domestic experience. There are no rules or statutory requirements other than those of the Companies Act. They find themselves attracted into trying to set up an organisation in London which can do things that their head office is not allowed to do; where the staff's experience is of a completely different type of banking to American; and where they can expand without being hemmed in by the federal and local statutory instruments of the U.S. All this tends to exaggerate the true role of the American banks. I do not think the American threat is anything as great as is often suggested. There are over 14,000 American banks: only three hundred or four hundred are involved in international affairs and only a handful provide competition. We are not really having to put up with the impact of the total weight of American banking.

In his seventieth year, with his retirement from active leadership of BOLSA approaching, Bolton issued a final Grand Review of the world as he saw it. His mind still has the stamp of youth: disdain for orthodoxy, enthusiasm for all that is new, searching, promising. On the one hand, he notes the failure of Europe to set a new example to the world and the threat that the United States, too, may lose coherence and strength. On the other hand, he responds to the challenge of new political models in Latin America, the one-party state, the paternalistic generals, the "puritan revolt"—all oddly familiar to European memories.

> A welcome, too, for the rebellion of youth against the frustrations of Western society. It is not in street disorders that he sees the threat of anarchy but in the continued acceptance of "nineteenth century liberal philosophies" by the political parties of the Western World. There are hints of his own preferences in the stress on indiscipline and irresponsibility, and his profound conviction that excessive government expenditure and undue wage increases are the basic evils of our time. Moving easily from political and social to monetary themes, he sharply condemns the efforts of most Western countries to hold down inflation by "the classical monetary techniques" of gold standard times; as he regards modern inflation as the result of governmental overspending and rapidly rising wages, he fears that control of the money supply or of credit expansion may produce economic recession without checking inflation. (This Keynesian view is now out of economic fashion, but that fact does not influence Bolton.)
>
> If this Review, published in March 1970, can be read as a kind of political testament, it shows perfectly the contrasting sides of the author's personality: profound pessimism, moral fervour, and vigorous pugnacity.

A decade has ended: it was optimistically baptised the Development Decade, but there is little evidence of any narrowing of the differences of income between the rich industrial nations and the developing world. Ten years ago it was believed in the United Nations and in some of the developing countries that the rich economies of the Northern Hemisphere would live in greater harmony and would have ample resources to finance the third world. This idea was greatly encouraged in Latin America, where it had particular significance, by the founding of the Inter-American Development Bank, which held its first constituent meeting in 1960, and by the launching of the Alliance for Progress the following year. A little later, in 1964, the developing world was further encourgaged by the dramatic confrontations of the poor and the rich nations, staged largely as a result of the inspired efforts of Raùl Prebisch, at the first UNCTAD conference; there were high hopes that the industrial nations would put the developing world firmly on the road to prosperity.

It was not foreseen that the 1960s would witness economic crises and monetary upheavals in the Western World that were to make direct aid on a major scale a practical impossibility. Not only has there been a drastic curtailment of official aid appropriations, but inflation and the rising cost of money in Europe and the U.S.A. have made it increasingly difficult for the developing countries to obtain capital; what they have seen in the latter part of the decade has been a growth in the cost of servicing their overseas debt. The progress in reducing trade barriers, especially those that now hinder the developing countries in exporting manufactured goods, has been negligible and in practice the rich have become richer by the exploitation of technological progress. It is hardly surprising that there is a growing disenchantment in Latin America over the capacity and the will of the rich countries to help the developing world over its difficulties.

It should equally cause no surprise, therefore, if the Latin Americans are increasingly dubious about the systems of government and monetary management that they inherited from the Old World. The institutions and organisations under whose control the world is entering the 1970s are, many of them, obsolete or corrupt and unequal to the needs and aspirations of new generations everywhere; this may be said, with at least partial truth, of parliamentary government, socialist dogma, the Marxist regimes, the churches, the trade unions, the universities, and most particularly of monetary systems. It is through the monetary system that official policy touches the citizen directly and where its weakness is most obvious; the greatest error of governments has been their unwillingness to admit that, by debasing thrift as a virtue and encouraging consumption rather than saving, by their own politically inspired over-spending and its concomitant of penal taxation, they have been undoing their peoples' faith in currencies and creating a growing distrust of paper money.

The decade has seen a constantly growing demand for money to finance government schemes; the rich economies are taxed to the limit and the official thirst for ever scarcer funds is in fierce competition with the needs of the private sector. This demand, combined with the falling value of money, has led to a general rise in interest rates without precedent in modern times and has threatened to disrupt the financial mechanism that has hitherto served the needs of the world's trade well enough. Faced with the threat that inflation would cause a breakdown in the system, the central banks and other authorities have attempted to check it by classical monetary techniques of the kind formerly used to curb a rising demand for credit—that is by raising the cost of borrowing, reinforcing this with physical limitations on bank lending, and consequently further accelerating the rise in interest rates. They have not been prepared to admit that the most potent factors in today's inflation have been government spending and rapidly rising wages. The traditional type of monetary restraint, in these conditions, has virtually no effect on consumer demand and government spending, but severely reduces liquidity in industry and, as experience in Latin America has shown, can easily lead to recession without checking inflation. The use of a crude monetary weapon to solve a political and psychological problem can produce the worst possible combination of circumstances.

The governments of the Western World have attempted to improve social conditions in their countries, but the inflationary consequences have weakened popular confidence in other values; I believe that a government when it is seen to be unable to maintain the purchasing power of a currency is regarded as unable to maintain the economy in general and —by inference—unable to exercise authority. Social behaviour is closely concerned with money; the citizen is less interested in political or economic theory than in what the money in his pocket will buy. No government can long sustain greater credibility than its currency deserves, and the paralysing effects of central bank monetary restraints, without a credible government policy to justify them or make them tolerable are giving rise to dissatisfied societies whose normal desire to work and progress is frustrated by lack of opportunity.

The generations born since 1938 find themselves members of a society with a brilliant record of technological achievement dimmed by the abandonment by its leaders of the old-fashioned virtues of thrift and sobriety. Restraint and repression have taken the place of example and authority; and the natural reaction is rebellion. Violence and its accompanying escape routes of "dropping out" and drug-addiction are sometimes represented simply as the revolt of youth against authority and the protest of the under-privileged against the elite. I do not accept that view: I believe rather that the young and the adventurous are frustrated by the vacillations and improvidence of their elders, and their protests are at the poverty of current standards and values and the lack of valid goals and opportunities. In these conditions anarchy is born, and the activists of the left and right alike thrive on resentments and discontent.

I would say that the heart of the problem lies, so far as the Western World is concerned, in the continuing acceptance by the political parties of nineteenth century liberal philosophies that have outlived the conditions that created them. The laissez faire attitude has degenerated into the permissive society, and an appeal to the moral issue makes no sense at a time when the almost total absence of a firm religious background makes it virtually impossible to define the word "moral". The lack of accepted criteria for decent behaviour has allowed political leaders to avoid difficult decisions and seems to be making for a comprehensive state of indiscipline and irresponsibility. It is this state of affairs that lies at the root of the revolt of youth.

These considerations are easier to discern in less rigid societies of more volatile people, such as those of Latin America, where dissatisfaction is more readily translated into activity. In Latin America frustrated and impatient populations have been championed by the armed forces, self-appointed watchdogs and guardians of the nations' well being. It is only a slight over-simplification to say that inflation and recession brought about by inept policies or corrupt administrations have been the basic causes of the deposition of more than one Latin American government in recent years. There have, of course, been other causes; I have already suggested, for example, that the Latin Americans, whatever their own shortcomings in economic management, have reason to be profoundly dissatisfied with the rich nations' conduct of world trade. Much of the frustration, the violent protest and the consequent political change in Latin America has been caused, perhaps indirectly, by the barriers to trade expansion maintained by the industrial nations and bitterly resented by the developing countries. The failure of the Development Decade and of the Alliance for Progress is not to be attributed to Latin American governments, but their inability to provide greater opportunities or more credible policies is a consequence of this failure and has resulted in the downfall of several.

The Anglo-Saxon world, with its unchanging political institutions, has regarded the Latin American republics with some contempt because of the comparative frequency of coups d'état and changes in political orientation. We do not make enough allowance for the fact that, in rapidly developing nations, social and economic changes happen more quickly than in the Old World. The Latin Americans are attempting to modernise their societies and to create systems of administration that will be more effective in the particular climate of each republic than the inherited structures and copies of U.S. institutions that have been intermittently in use since the early part of the last century and are still the ideal of "liberal" diehards. Europe, with its twentieth century background of war and destruction, has no cause to be contemptuous or patronising; there is much to suggest that the Latin Americans are evolving systems that will be enlightened examples to the rest of the world.

New political ideas are gaining ground in Latin America at the expense both of so-called representative democracy and of orthodox Communism. There has emerged a strong puritan element, more in the ethical than the religious sense, that is evident in the revolutionary governments of Argentina, Brazil, Bolivia and Peru; it has many points in common with the revolutionary political thinking of Mexico, which also has puritanical aspects, and it will probably evolve into a basic political pattern likely to prevail in Latin America in the future. The military men leading these new revolutionary movements are in certain senses Roundheads. They are interested in political morality, which has led them to dissolve the traditional parties, and in technical efficiency, which prompts them to find for Cabinet posts qualified men without political affiliations. Their attitudes are paternalistic and they do not subscribe to the idea that a nation should be free to determine its own corruption and perdition; nor will they allow any elite—whether landowners, industrialists, trade unionists, or foreign entrepreneurs—to enjoy unique privileges.

Sophisticated critics may say that the newest of new brooms soon becomes soft in Latin America; we may reply, however, that this contention is largely disproved by the example of Mexico, where a revolution has been in progress—real progress—for two generations and has now become a way of life. An important feature of the Mexican model is the omnipotent single political party providing a machinery that ensures that the Executive and the Congress pursue the same objectives and do not frustrate each other. It provides an effective means by which the policy makers in the party and the government can know the country's problems at village level. Among the revolutionary governments of South America, only that of Brazil has created a party mechanism, and it is a reasonable guess that we may see the official party, created in 1965, play an increasingly important role in the development of a new machinery of government. If that should prove to be so, the way may be opening for a smooth transition from a military to a civilian presidency which would preserve the principles that inspired the military intervention in March 1964 and ensure continuity of policy.

The nationalist element in the Roundhead revolutions may be seen in essence as a reaction against the concession of privileges, coupled with the habitual Latin American distrust of United States corporations and dollar diplomacy. This nationalism is an integral part of the revolutionaries' philosophy; the expropriation of foreign enterprises, as conducted in Peru for example, may have adverse economic consequences but it does enhance the sense of purpose behind the revolution. Nationalisation will make for political control over key economic factors, initially at the expense of foreign investment and economic growth; but the Roundhead governments are deeply concerned with the structure of their economies and with the technical reforms needed in their administrative and taxation systems, and new organisations will emerge. Their preoccupation with these problems has led inevitably to confrontations, not only with foreign interests, but also with domestic forces, including for example the priesthood.

The manifestations of decadent and ineffective governemnt in the Old World have prompted many people to ask themselves where and when the Puritan revolt would come. It may at first sight be surprising that it should appear in Latin America, although the trend supports my suggestion that by 1999 the Latin American republics—or at least the more advanced of them—would be world powers of decisive importance fulfilling Montaigne's forecast of their furture strength. Their capacity for austerity, acquired by long experience, and the determination of their Roundheads to break down social and economic barriers, give them a strength that the Old World seems to have lost. Their tradition of original radical thought and their readiness to reform both transplanted and indigenous institutions give them a flexible and pragmatic approach that Europe lacks. Europe is largely in the hands of politicians and political parties that are hardly more effective than those that have now disappeared from most Latin American countries. In the absence of the new vision demanded by the young, Europe shows no signs of achieving enough unity to assume a role of moral or political importance in the world. Will its civilisation prove to be one of those that have flowered and faded, as did those of Egypt, Persia, Greece, Rome and the great Caliphates?

The threat of turbulence in the United States is even more distressing; the deepening conflict between Black Power and white society is beyond the capability of the present political system to resolve. A very large number of negroes, who are citizens of the U.S.A. where the military draft is concerned, will return from Vietnam—where at least they had a purpose of sorts—to the aimlessness of unemployment in black ghettos. If, as I believe, violent demonstrations are the product largely of frustration and a national lack of purpose and self-discipline, the possibility that many negro GIs, skilled in the techniques of killing, may be deprived of the opportunity of satisfying work is a thought with deeply disturbing implications.

The distressing but unavoidable conclusion is that, since the end of the second world war, the U.S.A. has been so preoccupied with its newly assumed world role and so concerned not to lose any points in the contest of the "balance of terror", that the thinking-out of domestic policies has not kept pace with the problems. Similarly, United States monetary management has failed to meet the challenge arising from the greatly enhanced world role thrust upon the dollar by the demise of sterling as an international currency.

The close connection between the dollar and sterling systems makes it impossible to criticise one without condemning the management of the other; for political reasons, both have been abused and weakened in similar ways. But there is a vast difference between the low international standing of sterling as the currency of a nation that has lost power and influence, and the weakness of the dollar, which is the currency of the world's most powerful economy. The damage suffered by the sterling system will take a long time to repair in spite of the regained predominance of London as a financial market. Efficient and aggressive American industrial giants, however, have used the unique position of the dollar to purchase key situations from which to broaden their activities. This has led to a volume of criticism, but the European critics of the domination of the dollar miss the main issue. They forget the effect on U.K. monetary and economic policy of the post-war sterling balances, which at the 1945/6 dollar-sterling rate of exchange were equivalent to some U.S. $16,000 million.

During the immediate post war years a violent argument took place, particularly in Whitehall, about the merits and demerits of blocking the balances and, so to speak, starting afresh, or alternatively of allowing transferability inside the sterling area and a limited use of sterling balances held by non-Commonwealth countries. The spectre of creating an international depression by the withdrawal of the use of a key currency probably determined the decision broadly to maintain the sterling system, and any comparison between sterling in the 1940s and 1950s and the position of the dollar today must lead to some anxiety about the international monetary system's chances of meeting the problems of the 1970s. The sterling area was maintained partly by momentum inherited from the past, partly by a banking organisation of unparalleled strength and variety backed by the vitality of the City, and above all by the loyalty, however strained, of the Commonwealth countries that had traditionally used sterling. Washington has none of these advantages and already foreign banking claims exceed U.S. $40,000 million and are still rising. The dollar is being protected by historically high rates of interest, a complex series of restrictions designed to prevent the export of capital, and efforts, so far unsuccessful, to balance the budget and reduce consumer demand. The U.S. Administration will have to face far more frightening problems during the 1970s than the sterling problems of the past twenty years, and fear is a bad adviser.

It has been fortunate that the collapse of sterling as an international currency could to some extent be compensated by the growth of the Euro-dollar or international money market. The demand for capital, and the natural desire of the owners of funds to earn as much as possible with them without appreciable risk, have combined to create, with its centre in London, the only truly free capital market in the world. As any free market must, the Euro-currency market reflects in its interest rates the inflationary conditions prevailing in the U.S.A. and Europe and the consequent shortage of funds for long term investment; but its great virtue is that, in a period of growing government intervention, of monetary restrictions and the hampering of enterprise, it has flourished and has served a vital need. It will no doubt continue to expand as other capital markets of the traditional kind become less able to compete with one that offers to borrowers and lenders alike the advantages of a completely free system. In some ways it is a product of the age; a brilliant innovation that has grown uninterruptedly with the demands made on it.

I have mentioned in this Review several of the major financial controversies that will bedevil the 1970s—inflation, high rates of interest, exchange turmoil, declining savings and a growing disrespect for paper money—accepting all these disturbing phenomena as facts of life about which little can be done. We accept the fact that the gold standard and the gold exchange standard have disappeared for good, and there is in my view little likelihood of the dollar exchange standard being more than a provisional substitute. But since man instinctively clings to what he knows and no alternative has emerged, the financial machinery of the past will presumably be kept in being. In so far as it may be seen to be suffering from symptoms of collapse, the system will be modified and new devices will evolve. Thus a way out of the impasse may be found with the commercial banks' assuming the role of financing long term capital needs as well as the shorter term requirements of trade. If no essential distinction were made between short, medium and long term lending, and if the banks were made to assume the inherent responsibility, they would have to recruit the most intelligent and able members of the community, with the gifts and the courage to reconstruct and reorganise the monetary system despite the prejudices of hordes of economists, politicians and caudillos. Whether this forecast proves correct, or whatever other steps are taken to refurbish the system to meet future requirements, we can be sure that the City of London will play a vital part.

Appendices

APPENDIX I—SOME CITY STATISTICS

The banking revolution

The extraordinary growth in international banking in London is illustrated in Table I. This brings together the statistics for the accepting houses (big merchant banks), overseas banks and other business banks in the United Kingdom: for want of a better name, all these are called "wholesale banks" to distinguish them from the deposit banks (or clearing banks). Though the figures should be taken only as a broad guide to the main trends, it may be seen that their total deposits have risen from about £1,000 millions in 1955 to £3,000 millions in 1962 and to no less than £22,000 millions in 1969. This expansion reflects, partly, their participation in the fast-growing Euro-dollar market, partly their role in London's "new" money markets, and partly their aggressive search for business from British companies. Each of these strands is brought out in the Table—in the increase in their foreign currency deposits and advances; in the rise in their loans to U.K. local authorities (i.e. in the "new" local authority money market) and "balances with other banks"; and, finally, in the increase in their deposits from and advances to U.K. residents.

Table II gives a kind of photograph of the relative position of banks in 1969; these figures exclude transactions between one bank and another and so give a fairly good guide to their deposits from ordinary business and personal customers. It shows that the total deposits of the "wholesale" banks, whose business is largely international, has surpassed those of the great deposit banks like Barclays Bank, National

Westminster, Midland and Lloyds. The deposit banks, however, still have the bulk of the deposits of British residents.

Table III illustrates the growth in the numbers of foreign banks in the City of London—and in their business. London has far more foreign banks than any other of the world's financial centres: and the business they conduct has grown dramatically. In 1969 there were banks from no less than 42 countries represented in London either by a branch, or representative office, or affiliate. The large business conducted by American banks is apparent. Here again, the growth of the foreign banks, like the "wholesale banks" in general, reflects mainly, but not exclusively, their part in the Euro-dollar market. The large increase shown in their deposits from U.K. residents is also partly attributable to their participation in the sterling inter-bank market.

London—the Euro-dollar centre

Table IV illustrates the growth of the Euro-dollar market in London, which is easily the largest centre for this market. It shows that, in less than a decade, the foreign currency deposits placed with London banks have risen from the equivalent of about £1,000 millions to about £12,000 millions. By far the largest slice of these are denominated in U.S. dollars.

The City's capital market

Tables V to IX illustrate another of the great economic functions of the City—namely, the raising of long term capital for both British industry and overseas borrowers and the provision of a flexible market for trading in existing shares and bonds. In this respect, also, there has been a considerable expansion in the past generation. Table V shows that the market value of all the securities quoted on the London stock exchange has increased four times to about £132 thousand million since 1955. The London stock market also has a breadth and flexibility equalled only by New York. One way of looking at this is illustrated in the following two tables, showing the value and number of transactions each year. The number of transactions can amount to 20,000 or 30,000 on any one *day*, involving a turnover of perhaps £150 million or £200 million—again in a single day's trading.

The following Table illustrates the actual function of raising funds:

here again, the total value of issues made in the U.K. (mainly on the London Stock Exchange) has increased by four times since 1955. This is far more than could be accounted for by monetary inflation.

Table IX shows the rapid growth of investment trusts and unit trusts in England during the past decade: both these forms of organisation have played a big part in spreading the investment habit amongst sectors of the population that had previously not thought of investing in stocks and shares.

The City's Invisible Earnings

The Tables already mentioned have illustrated two of the main economic functions of the City of London—the servicing of trade and international finance through its banking system and in other ways, and the provision of capital to industry. But it is increasingly recognised that it has a third important function: the earning of income from overseas, which directly helps Britain's balance of payments. This arises because its services are used by people overseas: indeed, many of them are now primarily international in character.

These earnings are expanding rapidly. The final Table in this Appendix shows the general trend, and the earnings of particular sectors, namely insurance, banking, merchanting, investment and unit trusts, and "brokerage" (the Baltic Exchange and Stock Market, mainly). It may be seen that these earnings, in total, are estimated at nearly £350 millions in 1968 and it has been forecast that they could reach £500 millions by the late 1970s.

Table I

The "Wholesale" Banks—Main balance sheet items 1955-1969*

LIABILITIES	Dec 1955	Dec 1962	Dec 1965	*£ millions* Dec 1969
Deposits				
From U.K. banks:				
in sterling			366	1,483
in other currencies	209	460	684	4,116
From other U.K. residents:				
in sterling		431	1,046	2,103
in other currencies		76	90	397
From overseas residents:				
in sterling	626	1,096	1,356	1,080
in other currencies		960	2,042	10,484
Total deposits	960§	3,022	5,584	21,647†
ASSETS				
Balances with other U.K. banks	73	458	1,050	5,718
Money at call and short notice	266	280	282	249
Loans to U.K. local authorities	6	290	565	1,338
Sterling bills discounted	185	195	214	154
British Government stocks	352	475	512	430
Advances to U.K. residents:				
in sterling	121	445	912	1,230
in other currencies		15	136	632
Advances to overseas residents:				
in sterling	122	242	377	236
in other currencies		907	1,786	11,373
Total Advances	266§	1,608	3,210	13,472
Other assets		80	237	970
Acceptances		354	658	858

*This table brings together the figures for accepting houses, overseas banks and other banks (excluding the deposit banks) in the United Kingdom. The figures are intended only to give a broad indication of the main trends.
†Including negotiable certificates of deposit.
§Including unalloted items.

Table II

Banks in Britain 1969

£ millions	*Total Deposits**	*Deposits from Overseas residents*
Total all Banks	27,517	13,358
of which		
Deposit banks	11,814	459
"Wholesale" banks	15,558	12,883
Discount market	109	16
National Giro	36	—

*Excluding inter-bank balances.

APPENDIX I—SOME CITY STATISTICS

Table III

Foreign Banks in London and Domestic Banks

£ millions	*1955*	*1960*	*1965*	*1969*
Total Deposits				
Foreign Banks in London	263	701	2,558	12,508
(of which, U.S. banks)	(123)	(389)	(1,432)	(9,755)
U.K. deposit banks	6,685	7,407	10,080	11,814
Other British banks*	697	1,191	3,025	9,139
Deposits of Overseas Residents				
Foreign banks	156	541	1,815	8,735
(of which, U.S. banks)	(36)	(290)	(1,010)	(6,770)
U.K. deposit banks	n.a.	n.a.	429	459
Other British banks*	467	805	1,581	4,370
Deposits of U.K. residents†				
Foreign banks	39	160	743	3,773
(of which, U.S. banks)	(27)	(100)	(422)	(2,985)
U.K. deposit banks	6,685	7,407	9,651	11,355
Other British banks*	170	386	1,444	4,769

*"Other British banks" includes the accepting houses (i.e. big merchant banks), British overseas and Commonwealth banks (not all of which are British) and important affiliates of the deposit banks.

†Including inter-bank balances.

Table III (a)

Estimated number of Foreign Banks represented in London
(rounded numbers)

	1930's	*1957*	*1965*	*1969*
Foreign banks	80	80	100	150

Table IV

London—The Euro-dollar centre

Liabilities of U.K. Banks in Foreign currencies

	Total all currencies	*U.S. dollars*
1963	1,280	1,072
1964	1,786	1,566
1965	2,122	1,893
1966	3,022	2,727
1967	4,382	4,037
1968	7,131	6,402
1969	11,964	10,689

Table V

Value of Securities Quoted on the London Stock Exchange

£ millions	*Value of all Securities*	*Quoted Public Companies (U.K. and Overseas)*
1955	33,796	16,646
1960	45,068	29,149
1965	75,155	57,354
1969	131,679	113,219

Table VI

Value of Turnover on London Stock Exchange

£ millions	*All securities*	*Ordinary Shares*
1965	20,487	3,479
1969	30,391	8,713

Table VII

Number of Transactions (in thousands)

	All securities	*Ordinary Shares*
1965	4,361	3,417
1969	5,789	4,540

Table VIII

Capital Issues in the U.K.

£ millions

	Gross Issues		*Net Issues*	
	Total	*Overseas borrowers*	*Total*	*Companies*
1955	355	n.a.	275	269
1960	574	n.a.	481	431
1965	818	74	668	437
1969	1,234	233	879	613

Table IX

Investment Trusts and Unit Trusts

£ millions

	Investment Trusts Total Assets	*Unit Trusts Total funds*
1960	1,989	200
1965	3,145	522
1969	4,902	1,412

APPENDIX I—SOME CITY STATISTICS

Table X

Overseas Earnings of Financial and Allied Institutions

£ millions	1965	1966	1967	1968	1965-1967*	1966-1968
Insurance†	80	108	147	177	110	145
Banking	32	16	19	40	25	25
Merchanting	30–35	30–35	30–35	30–35	35	35
Investment trusts etc.	35	37	37	48	65	75
Brokerage etc.	28	27	31	42		
	205–210	218–223	264–269	337–342	235	280

*Three-year averages.
†Includes portfolio income.
Source: United Kingdom Balance of Payments 1969 ("Pink Book") H.M.S.O.

APPENDIX II—BOLSA UNDER SIR GEORGE BOLTON

by H. A. HOLLEY
Assistant Manager, Economic Intelligence Department, Bank of London & South America Limited

Origins and History

When in 1957 Sir George Bolton became chairman of the Bank of London & South America, the bank was already approaching its centenary year. Since 1862, when city bankers and merchants trading with South America first found themselves in a position "to carry out a project long desired, namely the extension of banking facilities through the employment of English capital in the important cities of Buenos Aires and Montevideo" British banking in Latin America had undergone a cycle of growth, maturity and relative decline.* A large number of banks capitalised and managed from London were established from the 1860s onwards to facilitate the movement of goods and capital between Britain and Latin America, and branches were established by one or more of these banks in every country but one on the mainland of South and Central America.

To combine in the right proportions adventurousness and prudence in an unfamiliar field of operations required exceptional talents, and by

*The quotation is from a statement at the Founders' Meeting of the London, Buenos Ayres and River Plate Bank. The full story of the Bank of London & South America and its component banks may be read in "A Century of Banking in Latin America" by David Joslin (OUP, 1963). A Short History of the Bank has also been published.

no means every bank established in that period survived the vagaries of rapidly but unevenly developing economies. Reading the history of these banks one is struck by the dominant role exercised by a few individuals and above all by the most dynamic of their chairmen in shaping the character and determining the fortunes of the banks that they administered: the continuing importance of this factor provides the theme of this study.

The present Bank of London & South America is in a sense the successor to most of the British banks in Latin America, but its direct line of descent is from the London and River Plate Bank* and the London & Brazilian Bank which were amalgamated in 1923 and the present name adopted. Avoiding speculative investment, the successful British banks made a major contribution to the development of the countries in which they operated by their stability in times of crisis. This was true above all of the London and River Plate Bank which alone of British banking ventures in the early days in Latin America never had to undergo reconstruction and never missed a dividend, as well as being the only private bank in the centres where it was established to redeem its entire note issue. Fundamental to the role of these banks was the financing of exports and imports—at first trade with Britain itself, then, through their own branches or correspondents, trade with other parts of Europe and North America as well as trade between the Latin American republics themselves; subsequently, as the domestic economies of the Latin American countries expanded with the beginnings of industrialisation, the banks increasingly helped to finance the domestic operations of local industrialists.

The first fifty years of the development of British banking in Latin America has to be seen as an integral part of that tremendous nineteenth century expansion of British overseas trade and investment which brought Latin America and other peripheral areas into the mainstream of the world economy and laid the foundations for their future economic development. It was British capital that financed the construction of the railways, docks, waterworks and other necessary elements in the infrastructure, either through direct investment or loans to national and local governments. Above all, Argentina as an investment field rivalled in attraction for the British investor the major countries of the Empire itself.

*London, Buenos Ayres and River Plate Bank from its foundation in 1862 until 1865.

Quite clearly in retrospect, the First World War marked the end of British commerical and financial dominance. Already by the beginning of the century, competition from United States traders was becoming progressively stronger and U.S. investments were moving southwards through the Caribbean and down the west coast of South America; the earliest U.S. bank branches in Latin America were established during the First World War. In the 1920s U.S. investments spread to all parts of Latin America and it was to New York that Latin American governments now looked when they wished to float bond issues. Though new British enterprises continued to be established, there was little net addition to the British investment stake in Latin America after the First World War, or in that of other European countries. There was still scope for the extension of British banking services, and the London and River Plate Bank continued to explore new fields in Colombia, Paraguay and elsewhere, but competition between British banks in many parts of Latin America was already becoming anachronistic. In 1918 the valuable connection with Lloyds Bank Ltd. was established when the latter acquired control of the London and River Plate Bank, and five years later it arranged the merger with the London and Brazilian Bank to create the Bank of London & South America.

Prosperity in Latin America in the 1920s—as in the larger world—was short lived. Nowhere were the effects of the world economic crisis which broke at the end of the decade felt more deeply than in Latin America, where export prices fell catastrophically and there was an abrupt cessation of the inflow of new capital. The traumatic experience of the depression years was to exercise a decisive influence on Latin American thinking for the next generation. For a foreign bank established in Latin America these years were especially difficult: as the economies of the various republics and their foreign trade contracted, the Bank of London and South America was deeply affected, but its stability was never in doubt. Many other financial institutions were fatally harmed by the events of those years, and among these was the other major representative of British banking in Latin America, the Anglo-South American Bank—which had itself absorbed many tributaries in the course of forty years of hectic development—and was deeply involved in the fortunes of the Chilean nitrate industry, then in the throes of a fundamental reorganisation. Although arrangements were made for the frozen assets of the "Anglo" to be taken over by a consortium of British banks headed by the Bank of England, it was eventually accepted that the only feasible solution was a unification of all British banking interests in Latin America. The business of the "Anglo" was accordingly acquired by the Bank of London & South America, which thus became the sole British bank in Latin America.

The Second World War and its Aftermath

The effects of the Second World War on Britain's economic position and on its relations with Latin America were even more disturbing than those of the first. As in the previous conflict, trade currents between Latin America and North America were strengthened, those with Britain and the rest of Europe weakened. Moreover, Britain's need and the aspirations of Latin American governments combined to bring about a liquidation of the larger part of the British investment stake in that part of the world. After the catastrophic fall in the foreign exchange earnings of the Latin American republics in the early 1930s the central government of every Latin American country (except Argentina) had defaulted on its external debt, and although arrangements were subsequently made for settlement of these debts, the lenders —to a large extent lenders in the U.K.—suffered heavy losses. The bulk of the rest of British investment in Latin America was in railways and other public utilities, and Argentina and other republics used a substantial part of their accumulated wartime earnings of sterling to purchase these assets. While direct investment in Latin America was resumed by the U.S.A. before the end of the Second World War, Britain and other countries of Europe were to make little new investment in the region until the later 1950s, while portfolio investment in Latin American securities could not be revived until the 1960s.

Within Latin America the economic picture had changed greatly from that of the 1930s. The remedy for excessive dependence on the outside world had been sought in accelerated import-substituting industrialisation, and this was to remain one of the main elements in Latin American economic policy. The mood was one of greater self-confidence and more assertive nationalism (of which the purchase of foreign-owned utilities was one facet), and in the early post-war years when commodity prices were still high the economic position of the republics—when compared to that in the 1930s—seemed relatively strong. When commodity prices fell in the mid-1950s and the republics became aware of their continued dependence on foreign capital and foreign aid, it was to North America that they had inevitably to turn. Spurred on by the clamant needs of their peoples and with an accelerating population growth, the Latin American republics were looking for partners in development, and Britain—chief economic partner of Latin America for most of its independent existence—seemed of all the industrial countries the least interested in filling such a role.

The change in Britain's economic position and the declining role of sterling posed problems of adjustment to all institutions in the City that were geared to overseas financial activity. What was to be the role of a British Overseas Bank in the post-war world, and in particular, of the sole representative of its class that operated entirely outside the sterling area? The bulk of British investment in Latin America had gone; trade with Latin America was but slowly recovering from its wartime decline. In reaction to the disappointments and losses of the thirties and forties, there seemed to be a positive prejudice in Britain against investment in Latin America, and as regards trade, the Latin American markets were regarded as difficult, unrewarding and exceptionally risky in comparison with those of the U.S.A., a reviving Europe and the familiar sterling area markets of the Commonwealth. Britain remained an important outlet for Latin American exports—and particularly for the meat and other temperate zone produce of the River Plate area. But, except by those financial or trading concerns which preserved their traditional link with the area, Latin America was virtually forgotten—by the government, by academic circles and by the public at large.*

The Bank of London & South America's own network of branches and that which it inherited from the Anglo-South American Bank and felt justified in keeping in operation, covered Iberia as well as Latin America from Central America to Punta Arenas on the Strait of Magellan, giving it representation in virtually all the chief commercial centres of this area. In geographical extension this network was unrivalled. Competition was, however, increasingly intense—not only from

*The neglect of Latin America in British universities stood in sharp contrast to the attention given to African and Asian studies. The situation was analysed, and recommendations made for its improvement—notably for the establishment of centres of Latin American studies in five universities—by the "Parry Committee" set up in 1962, whose report was published in 1965 ("Report of the Committee on Latin American Studies"; HMSO, London). Sir George Bolton was a member of the Committee.

U.S. banks that were vigorously expanding in the area but from domestic banks which had grown both in stature and numbers. These included in many countries state-owned commercial and specialist banks, and in the private sector powerful indigenous institutions often allied to major commercial and industrial groups, and in many countries a multiplicity of small local banks as well. Most Latin American countries could with justification be described as "over-banked". A foreign bank such as BOLSA still had a specialist role to play, particularly in relation to foreign operations, and could carry on a useful and moderately profitable business, but an impartial observer could have been forgiven for supposing that its future must almost inevitably be one of relative if not absolute decline.

The New Era of Expansion

In the immediate post-war years then BOLSA had to face a changing world—and one that was apparently not changing to its advantage. If it was going to assume a more dynamic role it needed both men and capital. At all levels, both at home and abroad, it possessed a nucleus of men skilled in the banking profession, but it also faced the problems arising from pre-war policies of recruitment and wartime losses. The bank's traditional strength preserved much of its domestic business overseas, although the heavy reduction in British investments had removed many of its old customers. Nevertheless it was, in the words of the Bank's historian, "left facing the more stringent conditions of the 1950s with old-fashioned premises, an ageing staff, and capital resources unchanged since 1936."

The situation was not one that the board, then under the chairmanship of the late Sir Francis Glyn, accepted passively. A move that was to be of great significance for the future of the bank was the initiation of a trainee programme, based to a large extent on graduate entry, to provide a new generation of managers for service overseas—a generation that was already represented at the highest level of the bank's management before the end of Sir George's tenure of office. The capital of the bank was raised in 1951 by the issue of a further £1m. to just over £5m. and £1m. also transferred to the published reserves. In place of the cramped quarters at Tokenhouse Yard, the Bank acquired a site at the corner of Queen Victoria Street and Queen Street and the new building was ready for occupation by the bank's head office and London branch in 1957. At the annual general meeting held in that year Sir Francis, then also chairman of Glyn, Mills & Co., announced—

> "I have felt for some time that the complexities and problems that arise in directing the affairs of the bank demand of the chairman more time and attention than I have been able to give them in view of my other responsibilities . . . I propose therefore in due course to give up the position of chairman . . . and my colleagues have intimated that they would wish to elect Sir George (Bolton) in my place."

In this choice the directors and shareholders had ensured that the task of renewal was to be carried forward with imagination and vigour.

The bank's potentialities for renewal and growth were in fact to be realised in a measure that few either inside or outside the bank could have foreseen. It was, however, with an eye not only to the future of BOLSA's position as an important British overseas bank but to the wider issue of Britain's relationship with Latin America that the new chairman moved to BOLSA from full time executive responsibilities in the Bank of England. The task in relation to BOLSA itself was a two-fold one: to define and strengthen the position of the bank in Latin America and to create for it a broader role as an international (rather than regional) bank transacting business in all parts of the world. Within Latin America this involved making the right deployment of managerial talent, modernising buildings, adopting throughout the branch network the appropriate methods of mechanical or electronic accounting, and searching for points of growth—either by expanding the network of branches or by diversifying into related fields of financial activity—as the economic situation and local legislation in the different countries permitted.

To carry out successfully this task of renewal in Latin America and to establish BOLSA as a truly international bank a radically new approach was necessary. This involved, fundamentally, a recognition that the international use of sterling would become progressively more limited and that it was in non-sterling finance—and particularly dollar finance—that the scope for the expansion of BOLSA's international operations lay. It was necessary to acquire dollar resources and the expertise for their deployment, and to build up a reputation as a bank concerned not only with the finance of British trade but of trade in all parts of the world. For a bank whose operations were increasingly based on the dollar and whose overseas branches were all outside the sterling area, dollar capital was needed and this was to be sought first by the arrangements made to finance development in the Caribbean area and then in the link with the Mellon Bank of Pittsburgh.

International Banking

With this new approach to the expansion of business and as a consequence of the decision to buy deposits at the going rate, BOLSA was one of the first banks to grasp the potentialities of the London Market in non-resident owned currencies other than sterling—usually known as the Euro-dollar market—and played an important part in its development, as of the subsequent market for longer-term funds (the "Eurobond" market). The role of London as the centre for these operations is described elsewhere in this book. Expansion of international business centred on London meant more staff—the foreign exchange department was naturally one of the first to be developed—more sophisticated equipment and more accommodation, and reorganisation of a head office structure devised to administer the traditional business of a British overseas bank.

By 1963 it was necessary to review the management structure of the bank in the light of its expansion, the increasingly diversified nature of its activities and future objectives. In this re-organisation the Bank and its, by then, numerous affiliates were viewed as a Group with the BOLSA board as the ultimate and co-ordinating authority, and the Chairman as its chief executive supported by three deputy chairmen. The post of general manager was discontinued and the broad activities of the Group organised in divisions under four (subsequently five) other executive directors. The former International Department was merged into a new International Banking Division designed to undertake much wider responsibilities than its predecessor. An increasing measure of autonomy was given to the local head offices in Argentina and Brazil.

Overseas representation of the International Banking Division—which handled a growing volume of business propositions that did not fall within the normal scope of branch banking—was maintained through its own representatives for different parts of Europe (both west and east) and North America, who were based as appropriate on London, Paris, Zurich, New York or Pittsburgh. A representative office was established in Mexico City in 1968 and in Japan in 1969. European connections were strengthened with the purchase of a significant equity holding in the well-known and old established banque d'affaires in Paris, the Banque Worms et Cie. In Britain, the representative office in Birmingham was converted into a branch to add to the provincial branches that had long existed in Bradford and Manchester. The International Banking Division naturally worked closely with the overseas branch network in Latin America, Iberia and New York, where the long-established agency had been converted into a branch in 1961—one of the two first foreign branches to be set up when local legislation at last made this practicable. A great expansion of business and need for larger premises led the bank to move from Wall Street to William Street in 1962 and back to Wall Street in 1970.

In the course of its development the organisation centred round the International Banking Division in London developed an expertise in foreign currency financing in support of trade and investment operations in all parts of the world. Sterling operations naturally became ever more closely confined to the financing of British exports and BOLSA was at a disadvantage here in that it did not have access to the free deposit money that made possible the cheap medium term export finance provided, under ECGD guarantee, by the clearing banks. But it could play a vital role in exporting, by providing the complementary "front-end" finance and also making arrangements for this to be combined with sterling finance in a comprehensive package, the "front-end" finance consisting of medium term foreign currency loans to finance down payments, local manufacture and other costs not covered by the ECGD-backed export credit. Such finance has been provided by BOLSA for as diverse undertakings as the steel industry in Spain, mining expansion in Chile, the sale of aircraft in Brazil, crude oil in Yugoslavia, and petrochemicals in Argentina. Lines of credit have been arranged to cover British exports to Colombia, Central America and Brazil, as well as a loan to the Inter-American Development Bank (IDB) which restored the eligibility of British suppliers to tender for contracts under IDB loans.

One promising development was the extension of contacts in Eastern Europe: finance provided by BOLSA over many years for Latin American countries' exports to Eastern Europe had provided the initial contact with official banks in that part of the world; with the decentralisation of the administration and financing of industrial enterprises in the later 1960s new opportunities arose. Following medium term financing operations in Yugoslavia, BOLSA arranged in 1969 a five-year loan of U.S. $15 million by an international consortium of banks to the National Bank of Hungary for the benefit of the Hungarian Aluminium Corporation—the first time since the war that money had been raised abroad for a Hungarian industry.

Another aspect of the Bank's work that expanded greatly was that carried out by its Investment Department. Besides its work in portfolio management this department was increasingly active in the Euro-bond market, participating in most major issues and holding an important position in the secondary market. In 1967 BOLSA sponsored the flotation of the Alexander Hamilton Fund (now the Alexander Fund), one of the earliest offshore investment funds, in association with the Bank of Scotland, Banque Worms et Cie and Svenska Handelsbanken. Another offshore company, the Stanhope Transatlantic Fund was launched in mid-1968. In the following year, various other investment funds were co-sponsored. A new investment company—Western Australian Capital Investments Company Limited—was also formed in Perth with the main object of investing in the shares of companies in secondary industries in that area.

The Link with the Dollar

The developments related in the preceding pages and simultaneous expansion in Latin America were carried out despite the debilitation of sterling. But for a bank based on London and operating largely outside the sterling area there were continuing disadvantages. Though the bank's sterling capital was augmented by fresh issues of shares, the use to which this capital could be put became increasingly restricted from the early 1960s onwards. Ideally, the bank needed a dollar partner to augment the resources of the Group. In 1965 this was achieved in the arrangement made with the Mellon Bank and Trust Company of Pittsburgh, whereby the latter, through its subsidiary Mellon Bank International, was to take up three million BOLSA shares, thus acquiring a fifteen per cent stake in BOLSA.

In the words of the Chairman—"The connection between the two banks offers obvious advantages to both parties. BOLSA, as well as obtaining an important amount of fresh capital in convertible currency, will reinforce the position it had been building up in the U.S.A. through its branch in New York by becoming associated with a bank which has powerful connections in the heartland of U.S. industry, and which has on its board the chairmen or presidents of some of the largest U.S. corporations in the steel, aluminium, petroleum, engineer ing, automobile and other industries.

The Mellon National Bank and Trust Company has, since its foundation by the Mellon family in 1869, absorbed or merged with numerous other banks both in Pittsburgh itself and in the State of Pennsylvania. Under U.S. banking law, it is, however, restricted in its operations to its home state. It is enabled, under the Edge Act, to transact a certain amount of international business through a subsidiary in New York, though in this respect it has necessarily been at a disadvantage vis-à-vis the big New York banks, which have wide networks of branches or associated banks overseas—in London and other European financial centres, and in some cases in Latin America as well. The two banks, BOLSA and Mellon, thus complement each other, and the financial link now to be established will provide the basis for a mutually advantageous co-operation in their business activities."*

The experience of the next three years was to prove the association most rewarding to both parties, and in 1968 new arrangements with Mellon Bank were approved whereby further issues of shares and convertible loan notes would be taken up by Mellon Bank; this further investment—amounting to some U.S.$20 million at prices current at the time the agreement was signed—was a signal mark of the U.S. bank's confidence in BOLSA, and if the whole of the conversion rights were exercised Mellon Bank's stake in BOLSA would be raised to a maximum of approximately twenty-five per cent.

The Great Rebuilding Programme

While the development of international banking centred on London had been taking place, a parallel expansion and diversification was undertaken in Latin America. One of the most important aspects of modernisation was the rebuilding programme. The branch offices in many Latin American cities were admirably sited in the heart of the business district, but often housed in buildings that were eloquent

*Article in Yorkshire Post, August 1965.

of the bank's history, inadequate for transacting an increased volume of business and inconvenient for staff and customers alike. In 1959 the Bank formed a small group of qualified architects within its own organisation. While employing local architects on each project, the formation of this group enabled the Bank to achieve better liaison with these architects and to conduct competitions for its major buildings.

In Brazil the branches at Belém and Belo Horizonte had been rehoused by 1960 and a competition was held for the design of the new São Paulo and Brasília branches, resulting in each case in the engagement of the distinguished Brazilian architect, Dr. Henrique Mindlin. The São Paulo building was built on the old site, and provided, in an eight storey building of contemporary design, accommodation both for the São Paulo branch and for the bank's administrative headquarters in Brazil which was moved from Rio de Janeiro to this more appropriate location. A new central office in Montevideo and new Group premises in New York were occupied in 1962 and the São Paulo building was the most outstanding of seven buildings in Argentina, Brazil, Chile and Uruguay completed in the following year.

In due course most other branch offices were rehoused or existing premises remodelled, and by 1970, of ninety-nine offices occupied by the bank itself, no less than ninety-four had been housed in new or modernised premises. The major rebuilding operation was, however, the new central office in Buenos Aires. In 1959 intensive studies were conducted by the bank's officers and architects to consider the requirements of the new building—in terms of functional efficiency rather than traditional bank building design—and an architectural competition was held in the following year. A staff of some 1,500 working in many departments with varying degrees of relationship and together comprising both the administrative headquarters in Argentina and what is probably the largest private bank branch established in any foreign country had to be accommodated; an important factor to be taken into account was the exceptional cash movement in Buenos Aires, and provision had to be made for no less than one hundred and thirty-three cashiers. These problems found a brilliant solution in the winning design by a firm of Buenos Aires architects: this abolished the banking hall as such, by conceiving the whole building as a huge banking hall within which there were no conventional floors, but a series of interconnecting levels affording easy communication between departments and permitting impressive interior vistas. The exterior is no less unconventional, its strikingly modern elevation contrasting strongly with the classical façades of the more traditional buildings in the banking quarter of the city. The foundation stone of the new building, which has since become an accepted feature of the city and may be said to have made an original contribution to design in a specialised field of architecture, was laid by HRH The Duke of Edinburgh during his visit to Argentina in March 1962 and the building opened by Sir George Bolton in July 1966.*

Expansion in Latin America

While the bank was modernising both its image and its capacity for efficient service in the principal centres of operation, it was also examining the scope for expansion, both in geographic coverage and function. Both tasks placed heavy demands on the bank's capital resources. An early move under Sir George's chairmanship was the decision to approach a well-established institution outside the United Kingdom that might combine with BOLSA to take full advantage of the opportunities for the expansion of business in the Caribbean area. Canada had long had commercial interests throughout Central and South America as well as in the West Indies. In 1958, therefore, the bank came to an agreement with the Bank of Montreal whereby a joint organisation would be set up to explore banking possibilities in the West Indies and to develop to the fullest extent BOLSA's existing branch network in Central America and adjacent South American countries. As a result of these negotiations the Bank of London & Montreal—BOLAM as it became known—was established with a paid up capital of £5 million, consisting in equal proportions of capital subscribed by the Bank of Montreal and working capital and premises of BOLSA in Colombia, Ecuador, Venezuela, El Salvador, Guatemala and Nicaragua.

The new bank opened its head office in Nassau, Bahamas, in October 1958 and pursued a vigorous course of expansion, establishing itself in Jamaica, Trinidad and Honduras—where it was the first branch of a

*On the first day over twenty thousand people visited the building. The architects were Sres. Sánchez Elia, Peralta Ramos and Agostini in association with Sr. Clorindo Testa. A model of the new building was accepted for exhibition at the 1963 Summer Exhibition of the Royal Academy in London.

foreign bank to operate—and subsequently in Panama, and setting up new branches and agencies in countries where it was already represented. In Venezuela the branch in Caracas was merged with that of the Banco la Guaira C.A. to form Banco la Guaira Internacional—a company in which BOLAM thus took a substantial minority interest and representation was secured in Costa Rica through a local subsidiary. In 1964 Barclays D.C.O., already long established in the Caribbean, became third equal partner in BOLAM whose subscribed capital was thus raised to £7½ million, and over the next five years this pooling of the expertise, resources and international connections of the parent banks was to prove effective, despite increasing competition, in developing commercial banking and related financial activities on the mainland and islands, as well as a substantial international business based on the head office in Nassau. After twelve years of progress, during which the number of BOLAM's offices rose from 13 to 56 in ten countries of South and Central America and the Caribbean, it was decided that future development could best be planned with a realignment of responsibilities; an agreement was reached early in 1970 whereby BOLAM, with its branches on the mainland of Latin America, would become a wholly-owned subsidiary of BOLSA, in which the other two partner banks would acquire a corresponding shareholding.

In the other traditional centres of Latin American operations BOLSA itself pursued a similar path of expansion. The defensive reaction that had led in the years after the war to the closure of branches in a number of countries, including Uruguay and Brazil (as late as 1955) was rejected in favour of a determination to make branches economic and to expand where circumstances and local legislation permitted. In the metropolitan areas of Buenos Aires, Montevideo, Santiago, Asunción, Lima and other cities additional branches or agencies were opened to attract new customers and give wider service. Strengthening the branch banking business in Latin America and Iberia meant not only widening territorial coverage, but competing vigorously in traditional fields of commercial banking activity, providing new services and equipping branches to carry out these tasks. Buenos Aires followed London in becoming "computerised"; its new branches included one in the well-known department store of Harrods in the heart of the city; it organised a campaign to promote "non-traditional" exports, and introduced the credit card to Argentina.

As well as strengthening and extending its commercial banking network and business in Latin America, BOLSA in the late 1950s set about diversifying into merchant and investment banking. A major development was the acquisition in 1960 of the share capital of the old-established merchant banking firm of Balfour Williamson & Company Ltd. Founded in Liverpool in 1851 by three young Scotsmen, it began its activities in trade with Chile, and in more than a century of existence there was hardly any form of economic activity in which it and its associated companies had not at some time participated. The Balfour Williamson group with its wide experience and representation made it a natural complement to the Bank, enabling it to concentrate on banking business and to leave to Balfour Williamson the financial and trading operations that are more suited to a merchant banking group.

The group, which consisted of twenty-three companies operating in eight different countries, was reorganised and refinanced during the next few years. Most of the trade investments—including the important trading subsidiaries operating in the west coast republics of South America—were eventually transferred to the bank.* Balfour Williamson & Co. Ltd. ceased to be the holding and management company for the Balfour Williamson group and became an operating subsidiary of the BOLSA group with its own subsidiaries and offices in various parts of the world, and specialising in international financing and confirming operations at short and medium-term, with strong emphasis on Europe, Africa, Australasia and the Caribbean, as well as its more traditional area of the Americas. Balfour Williamson and the other export houses make a significant contribution to Britain's balance of payments, directly by their own overseas earnings of profits, commissions and interest, and indirectly by stimulating exports. The committee which was appointed in 1966 to survey the field of Britain's invisible earnings included among its members both Sir George Bolton and the Hon. R. D. Campbell, Managing Director of Balfour Williamson & Co. Ltd.

*With the association between BOLSA and the Mellon Bank it became necessary, in compliance with U.S. banking legislation, for Balfour Williamson to withdraw from domestic operations in the U.S.A. Following the disposal of its trading interests, the New York subsidiary of Balfour Williamson confined its business to the provision of confirming and financing services for the international movement of goods.

Investment Banking

Within the Latin American republics themselves the 1950s and 1960s brought the opportunity for diversification outside the sphere of traditional commercial banking. In some countries banking legislation made it necessary—even if it had not on other grounds been desirable—to establish new institutions to carry out functions, other than those of a narrowly defined commercial banking. In the more sophisticated Latin American countries new financial institutions had to be evolved to finance the production and sale of durable consumer and capital goods produced by a more mature industrial economy. There was need also for institutions in the private sector that would help to develop incipient capital markets by the underwriting and placement of shares and other means of mobilising medium and long term money for development from sources both national and international.

The name by which such institutions are most frequently known—financieras—covers a diverse range of activities. The earliest venture of BOLSA in this field was the Compañia Financiera de Londres which opened for business in Buenos Aires in 1961. The fulfilment of the early promise of the Financiera was naturally dependent on local business conditions, and from 1962 onwards there was a period of renewed political and economic difficulties for Argentina that was not brought to an end until 1966 when a new political regime was established and a far-reaching series of reform and stabilisation measures introduced in the following year. In this improved economic climate losses were quickly eliminated and the Financiera was able to play a part in helping to channel into industrial investment the inflow of capital into Argentina that followed this improvement. In 1967 the growth of operations in the interior of the country led to the establishment of a branch in Rosario, to be followed by others in Córdoba and Mendoza in 1969. Business, and profitability, continued to expand in that year, and among its wide-ranging activities the Financiera was a prime mover in the development of the local acceptance market.

In Brazil, too, the improved political and economic situation of the later 1960s provided favourable conditions for expansion in a similar direction. One important aspect of the overhaul of the country's financial and monetary system undertaken by the regime that came to power in 1964 was legislation defining the roles to be played by different kinds of financial institutions, and in particular drawing a distinction between the roles of investment banks and finance houses. There was thus established a kind of "three-tier" sytsem of financial institutions in the private sector, and it was clearly of advantage to be able to operate at all three levels. With the aim, therefore, of embarking on a more broadly-based expansion of the Bank's business in Brazil, an agreement was reached in 1967 to set up an investment bank jointly with the Bozano Simonsen group, each party holding a fifty per cent interest in the voting equity capital. Bozano Simonsen's principal interests had hitherto consisted of two finance companies with an exceptional record of growth. With the new association one of these companies was converted into the investment bank while the other continued to function as a finance company. The two organisations could together offer their clients the widest range of services, including underwriting, distribution of securities, capital market operations, medium term financing and hire-purchase. A close working relationship with BOLSA's branches was developed, and the ability and enterprise of the local board, together with the financial backing which BOLSA was able to provide, were largely responsible for its encouraging and profitable start.

Other financieras of a rather different kind in which the Bank has taken an interest—though in these cases necessarily only a minority one—are the development finance companies that were established, especially in the northern republics of South America and in Central America from the late 1950s onwards. These development finance companies were created as a kind of private sector counterpart to the official development banks. The most important investments which BOLSA has made in this type of financiera have been in two of the most successful, the Corporación Financiera Colombiana and the Corporación Financiera Nacional in Bogotá and Medellín, Colombia. Other financieras in which BOLSA has an interest are in Peru and Mexico, while BOLAM has similar investments in Central America and elsewhere. An organisation similar in purpose though much broader in scope than any of the local private development banks is the ADELA Investment Company, of which Sir George Bolton is a director and a member of the executive committee. ADELA was formed in 1964 as a multi-national private investment banking organisation designed to mobilise resources for channelling into productive private enterprises in Latin America. Its shareholders are two hundred and thirty-nine major industrial and financial institutions in Western Europe, the U.S.A., Canada, Japan and Latin America; there are fifteen U.K. shareholders which are co-ordinated by BOLSA.

With the development of international banking business based on London, BOLSA's dependence on Latin America has been considerably diminished, but as the developments outlined above indicate, this has not meant any diminution of interest; it is in relative, not absolute terms that Latin America has become less important to BOLSA. With all their vicissitudes, the Latin American republics had, with few exceptions, recorded substantial, if rarely steady, economic advance during the 1960s. Despite their vulnerability as primary producers and the strains imposed by industrialisation, progress was also made towards stability. Despite the rapid growth of population in nearly all the republics, economic growth was nearly everywhere outpacing this—even if it was still far from satisfying the aspirations of their peoples. There were signs, too, that Latin America was finding its own solutions to political problems. Viewed against the background of events in the other developing countries in Africa and Asia, Latin America's achievements and potentialities became increasingly significant for the western world. It was in no small measure due to the activities of Sir George Bolton that by 1970 it was no longer necessary to remind British exporters, government officials and academics of that fact.

The progress of the bank itself may be summed up in a few figures: an increase in issued capital from £5.05 million at the end of 1957 to £21.1 million at the end of 1969, in net members' funds from £9.3 million to £33.6 million, and in gross group assets from £146 million to £790 million. Through twenty-four principal subsidiary and associated companies the group participated in all aspects of banking and related financial services. The number of overseas banking offices maintained by it and its subsidiaries in Europe and the Americas had more than doubled to one hundred and forty-four. Increasing competition in all aspects of activity becomes evident, but competition is a condition of progress, and a rejuvenated BOLSA has no doubt of its ability both to meet it and to create it for others, and to pioneer fresh fields of financial activity.

INDEX

INDEX

INDEX

www.ingramcontent.com/pod-product-compliance
Lightning Source LLC
LaVergne TN
LVHW011127300926
849160LV00008B/552